Editor in Chief
ANTWAN 'ANT' BANK$

Managing Editor
TAYVO BANK$

Photographers
Silvio Saurez
Paul Lawson

Cover design
SK7 Studios

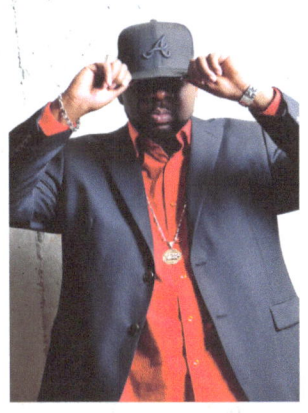

VIP INK Publishing Group
www.PrintHouseBooks.com

ISBN: 978-0-997-8116-43

Retailers call **1-800-937-8200** to place wholesale orders. Please have above ISBN available when calling.

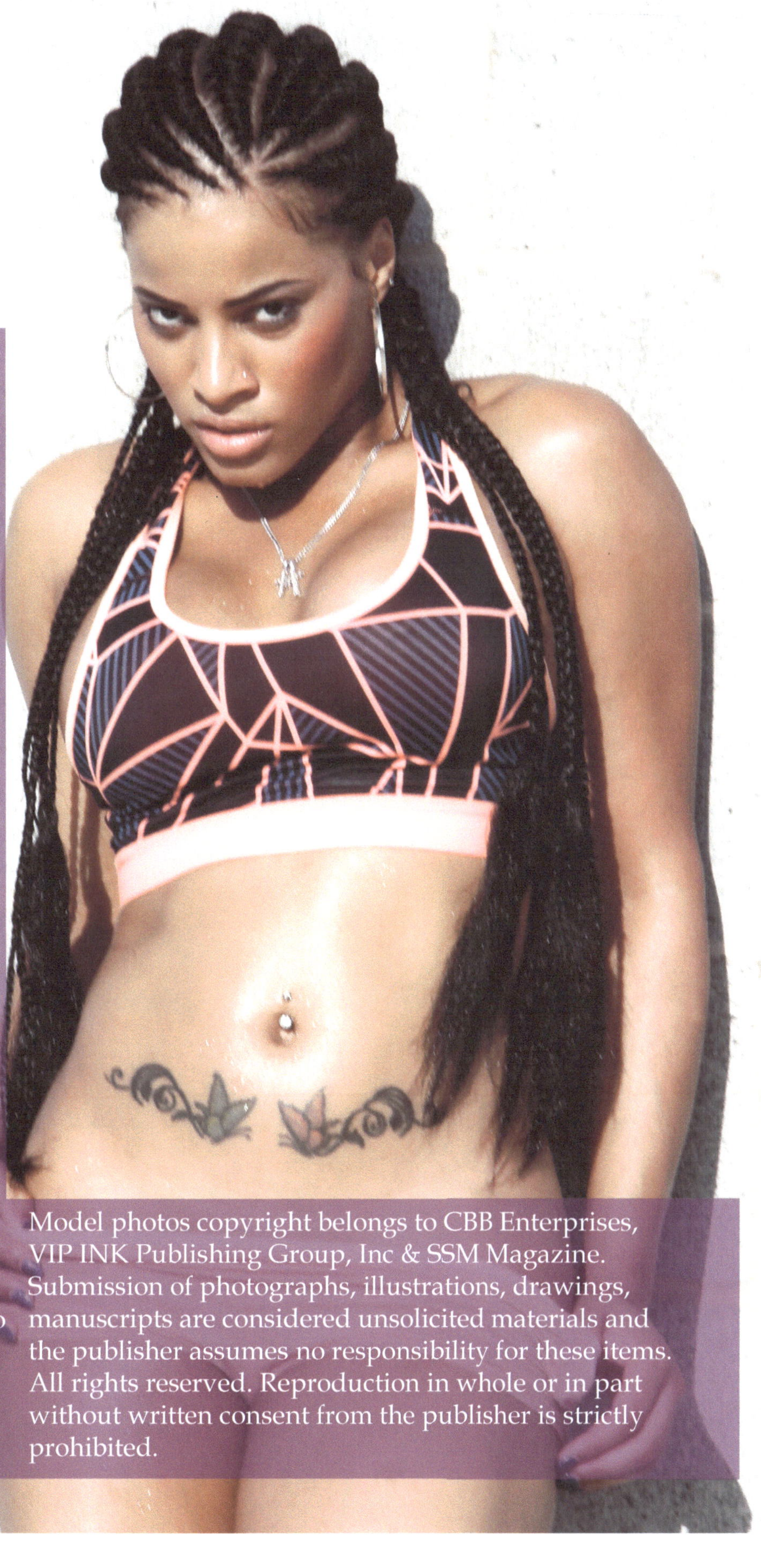

I0493796

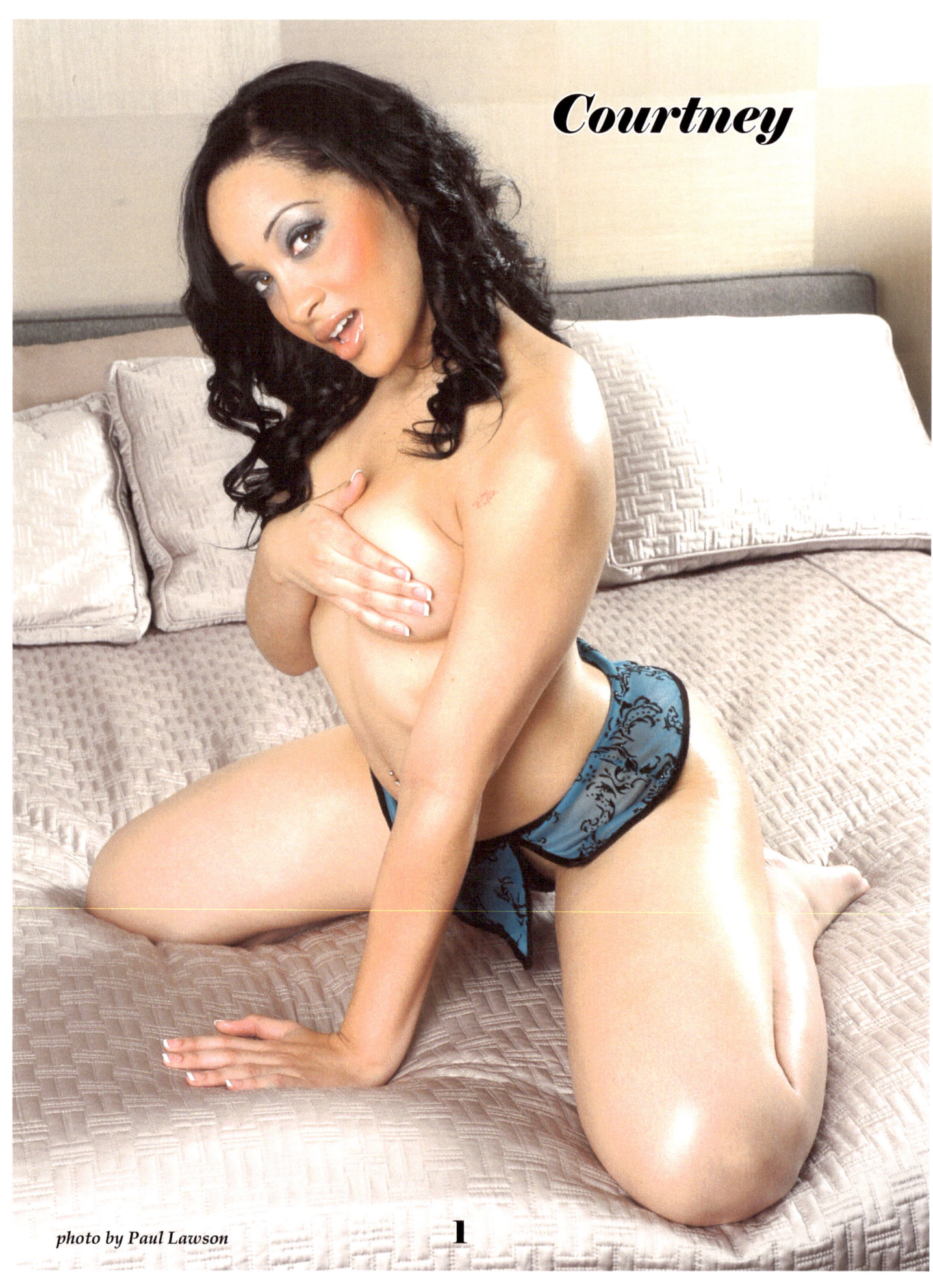

Courtney

1

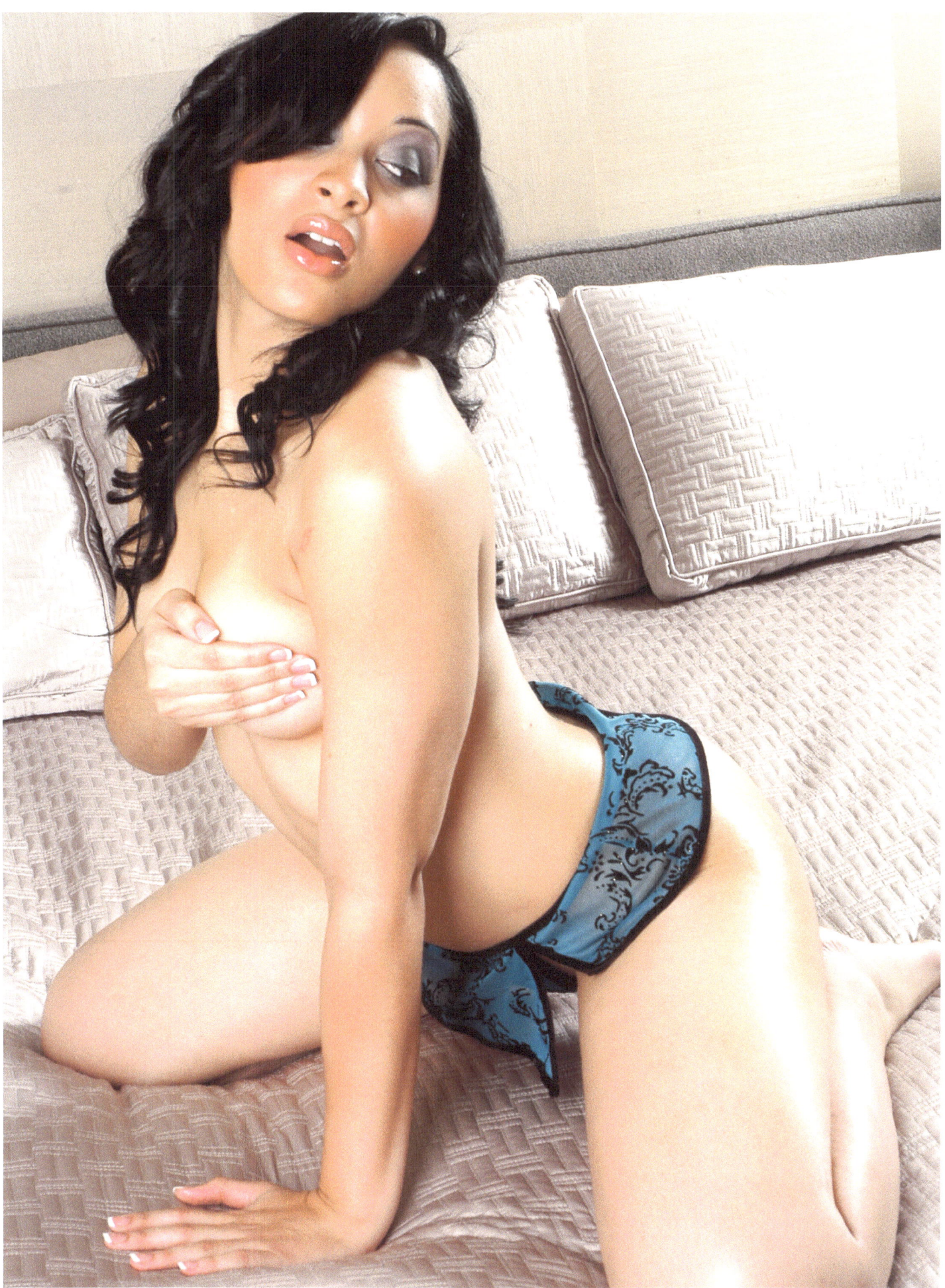

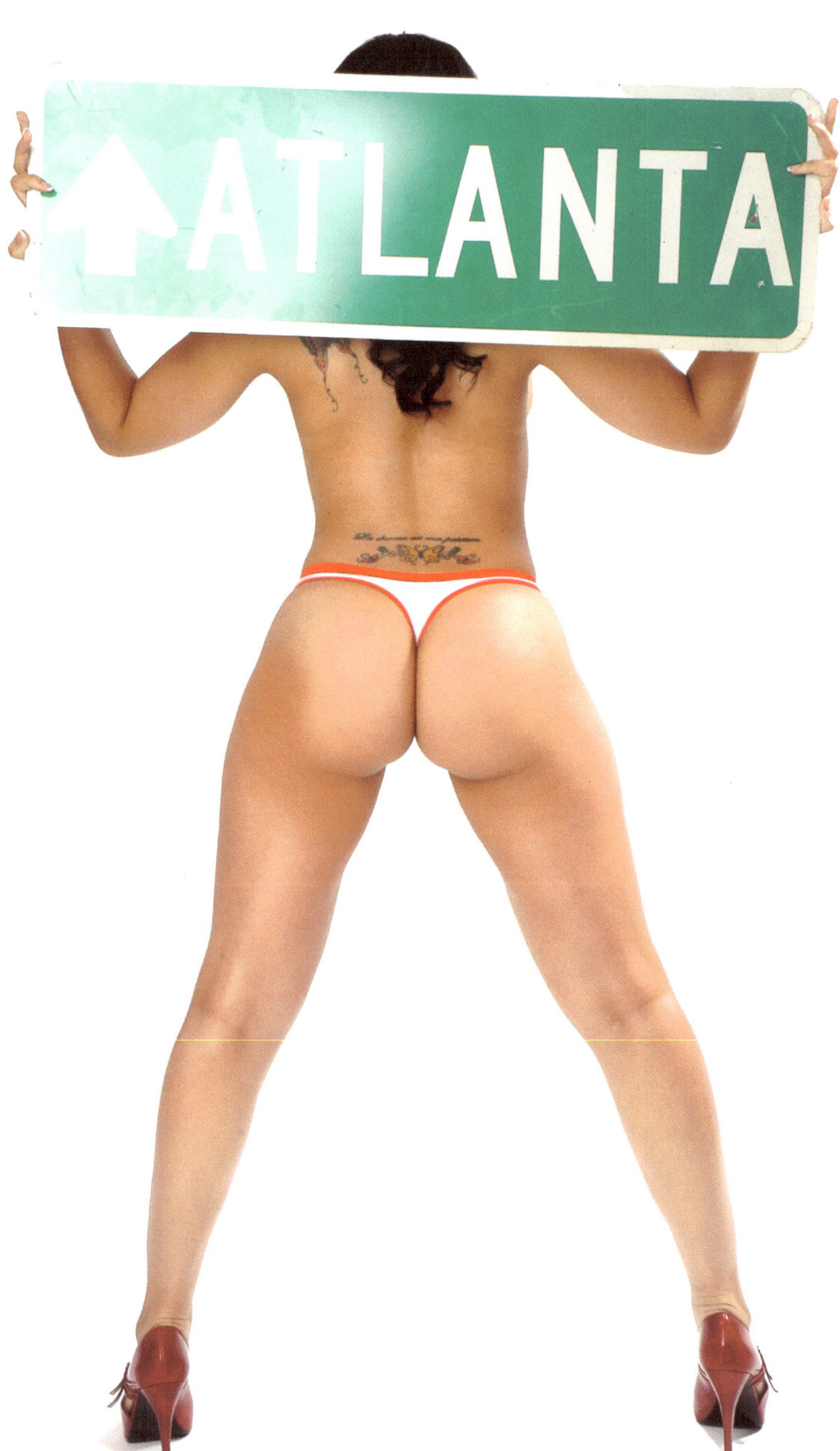

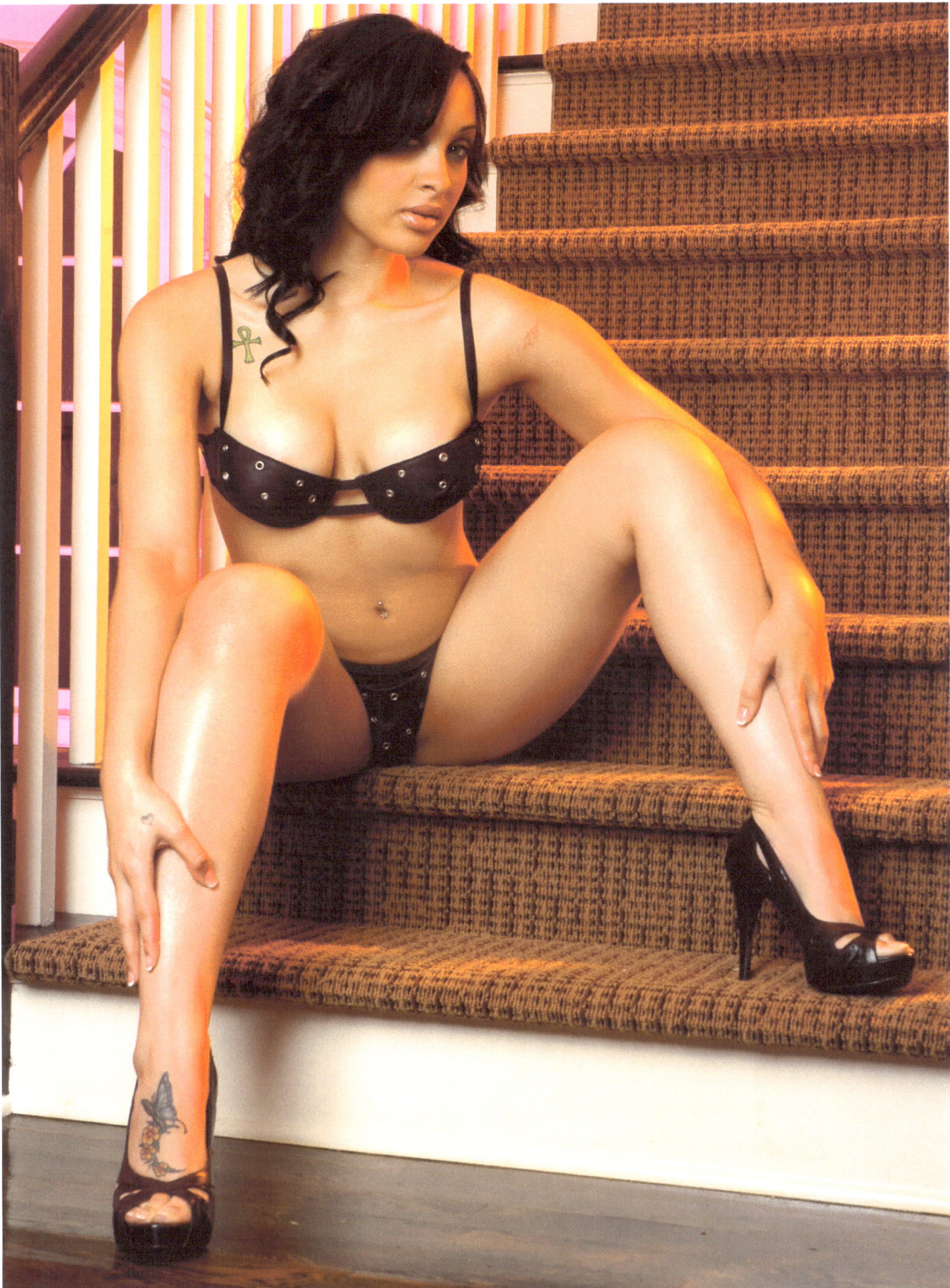

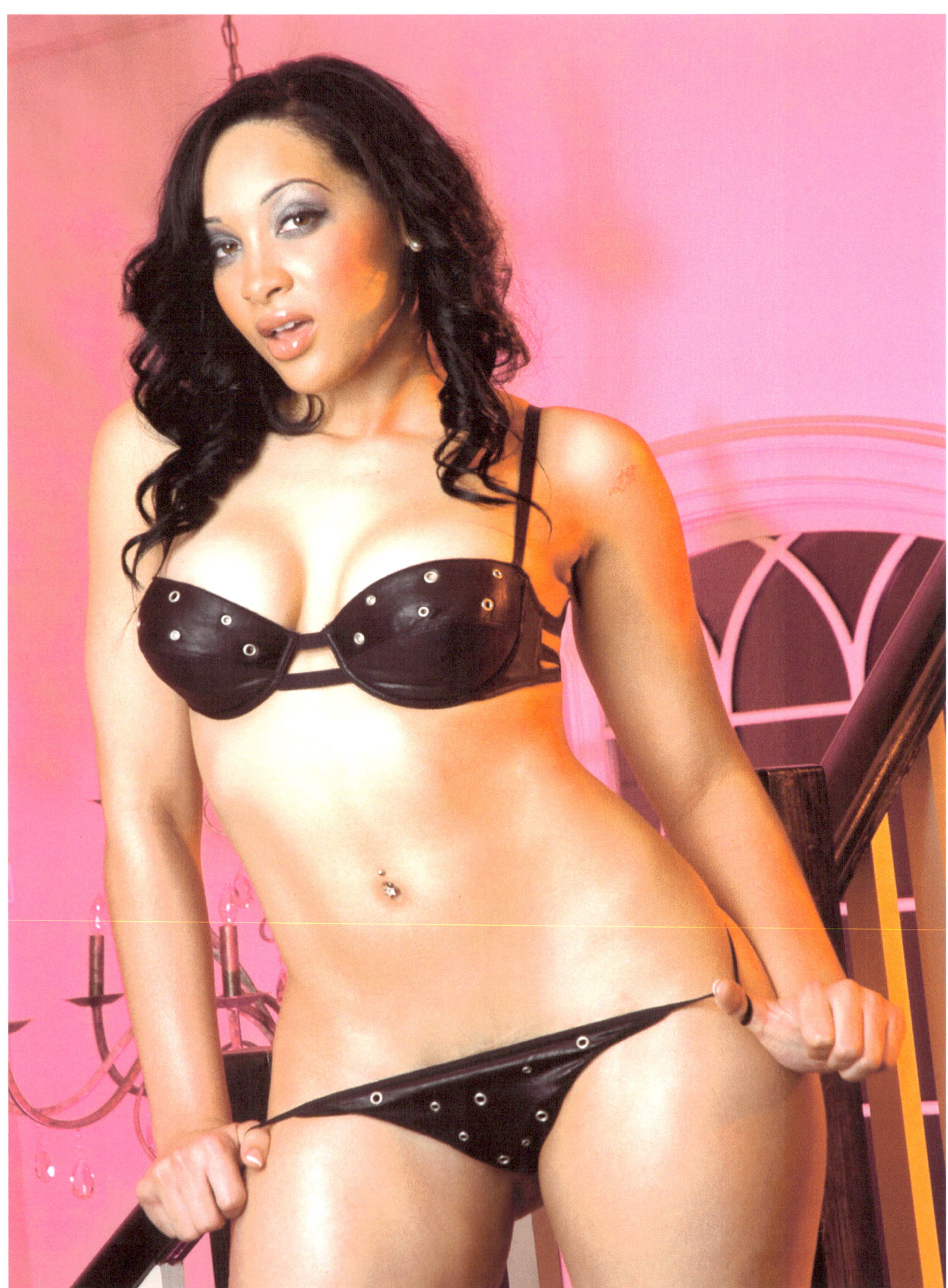

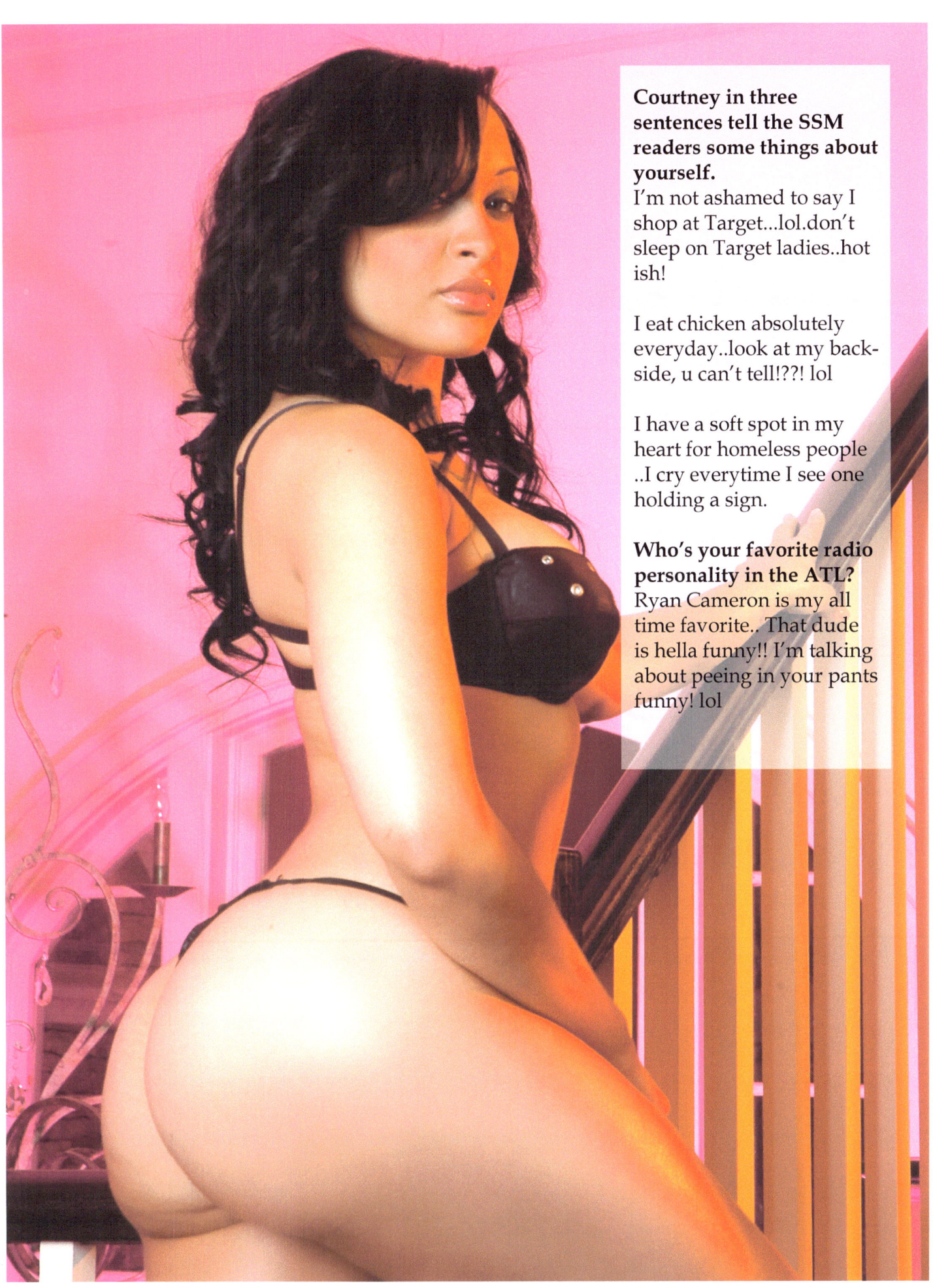

Courtney in three sentences tell the SSM readers some things about yourself.
I'm not ashamed to say I shop at Target...lol.don't sleep on Target ladies..hot ish!

I eat chicken absolutely everyday..look at my backside, u can't tell!??! lol

I have a soft spot in my heart for homeless people ..I cry everytime I see one holding a sign.

Who's your favorite radio personality in the ATL?
Ryan Cameron is my all time favorite.. That dude is hella funny!! I'm talking about peeing in your pants funny! lol

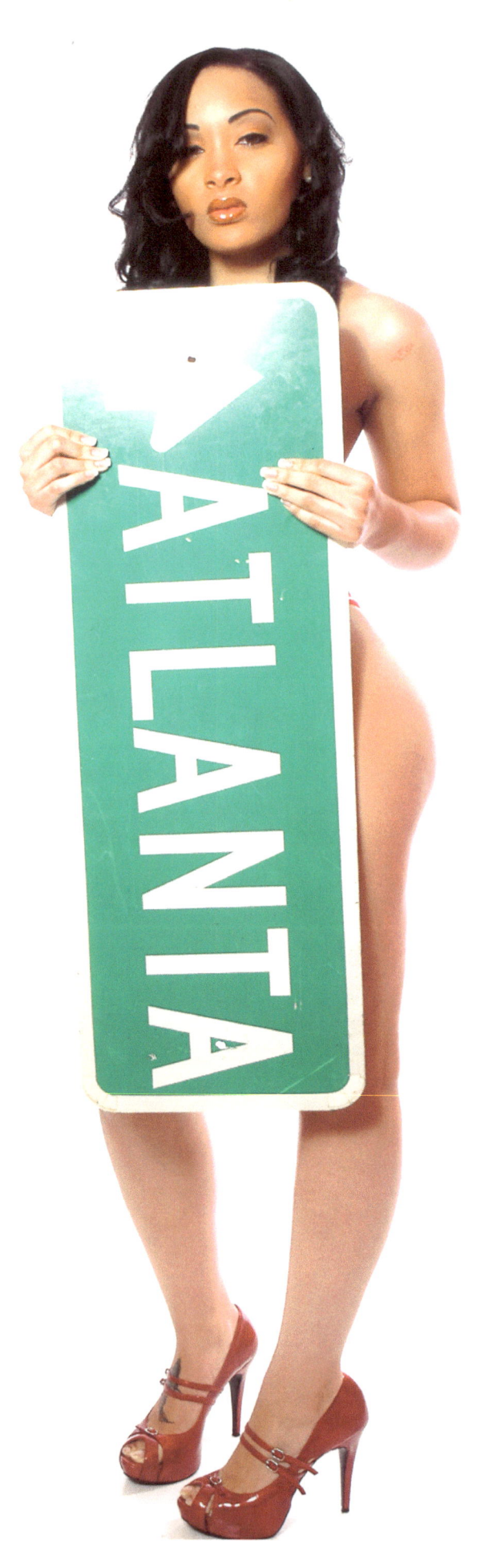

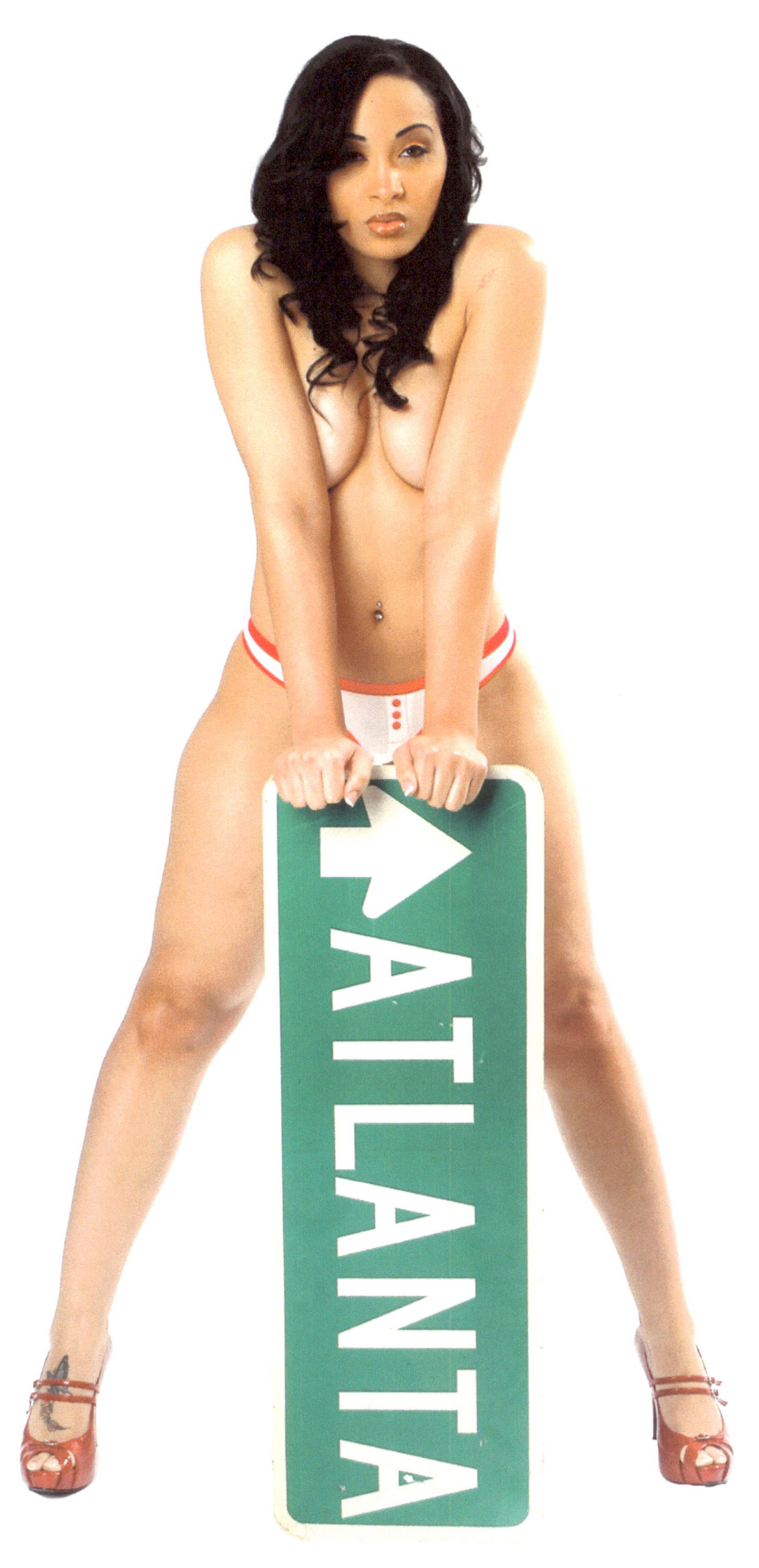

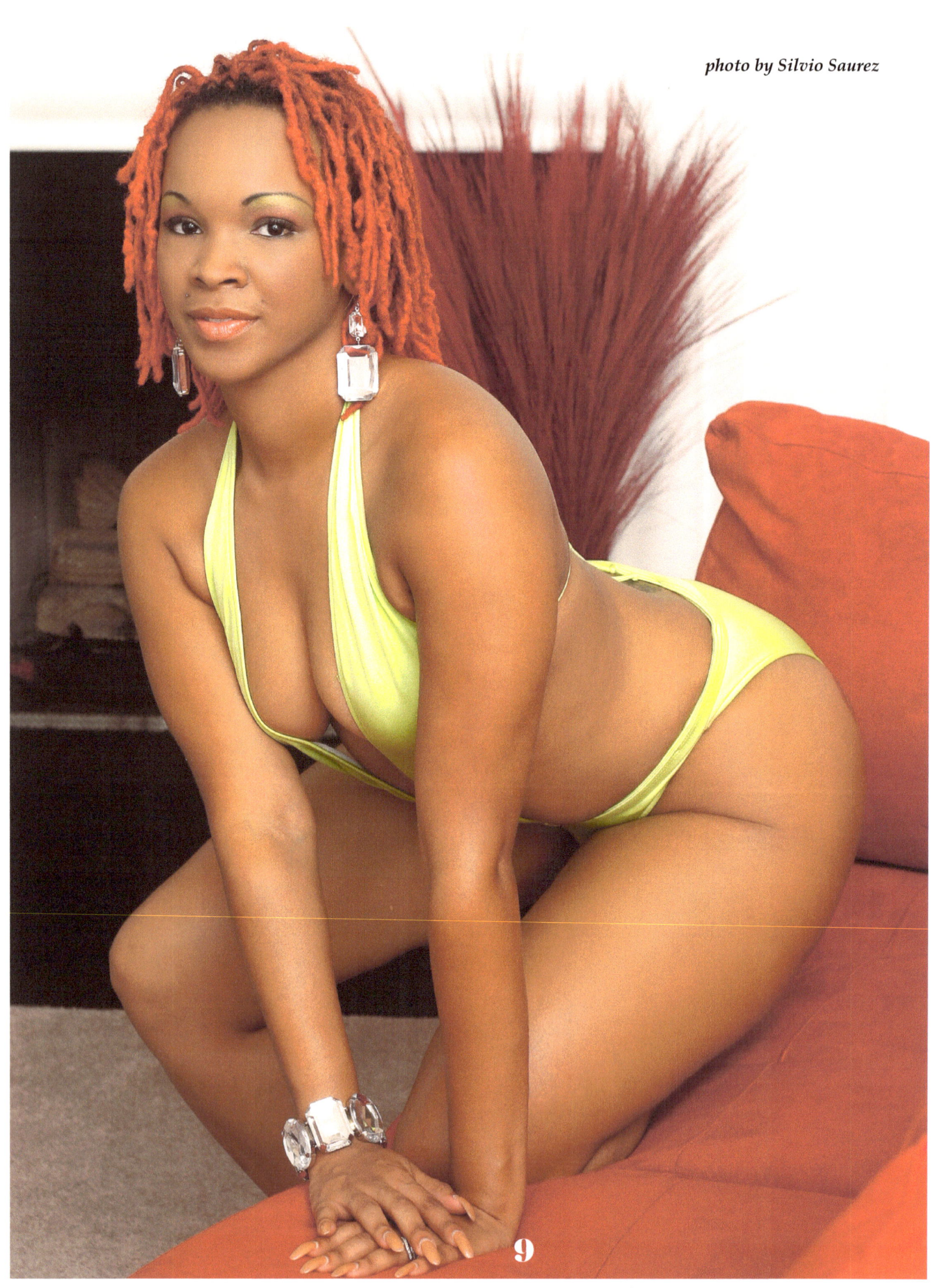

9

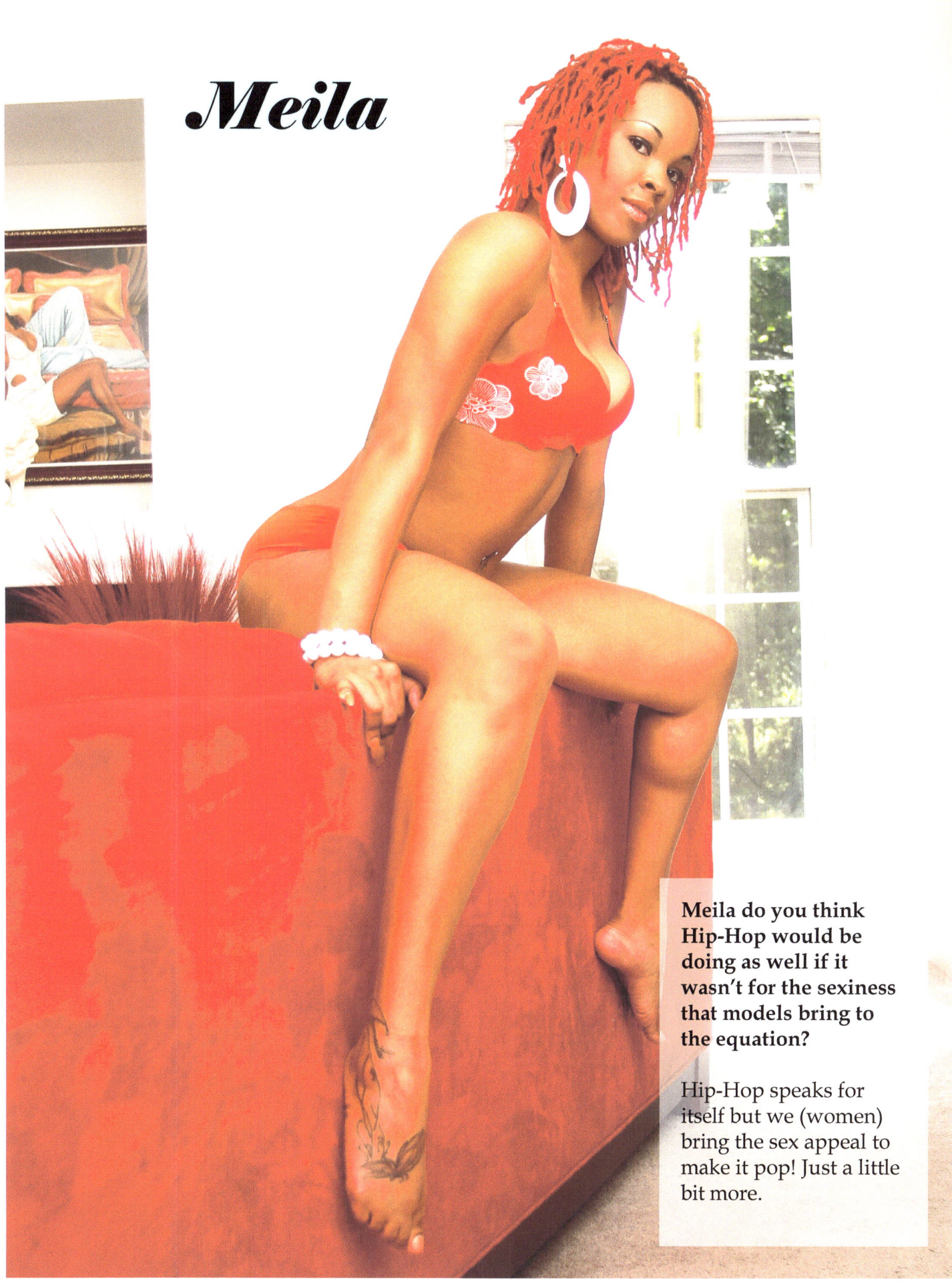

Meila

Meila do you think Hip-Hop would be doing as well if it wasn't for the sexiness that models bring to the equation?

Hip-Hop speaks for itself but we (women) bring the sex appeal to make it pop! Just a little bit more.

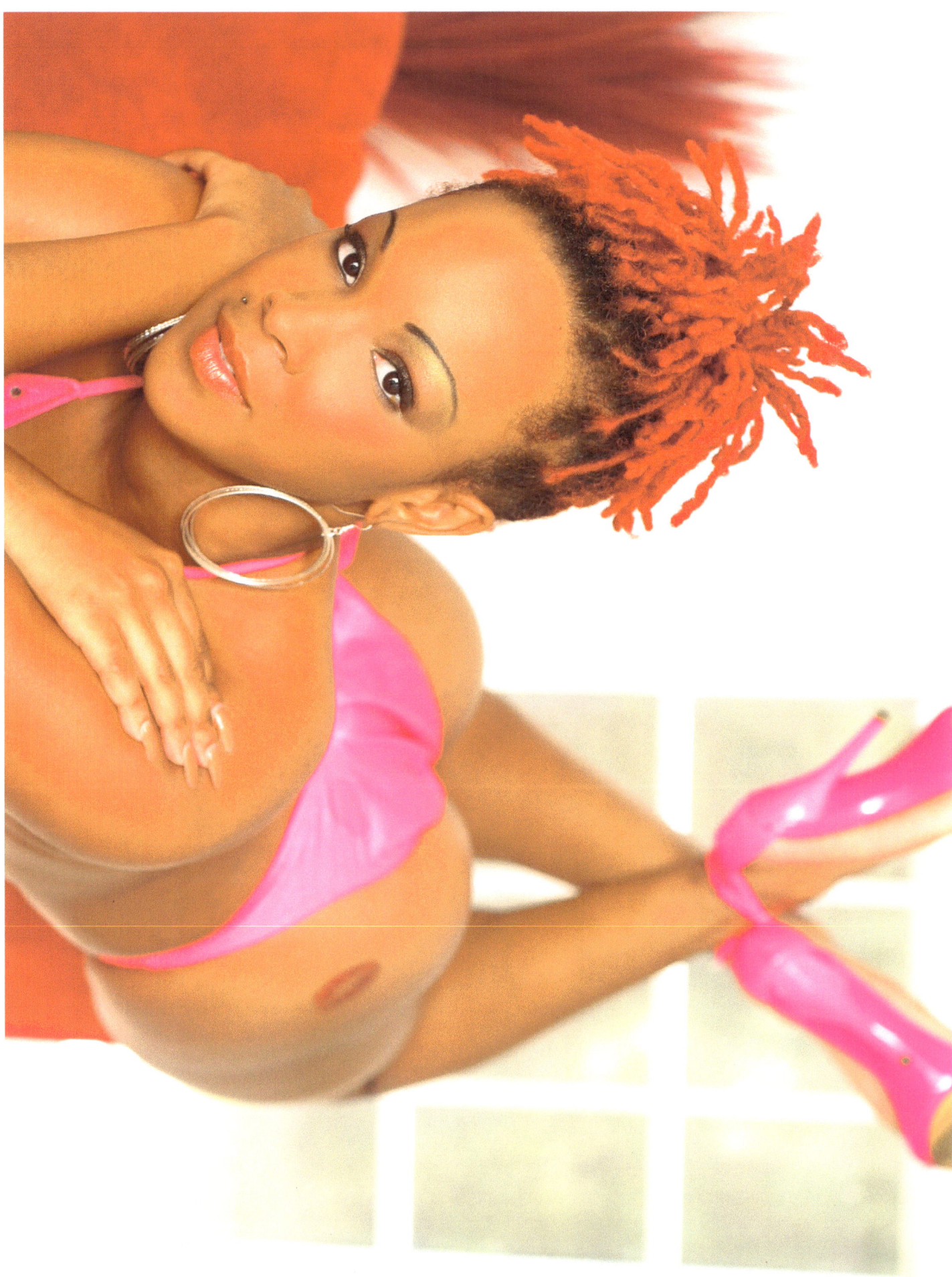

Drake - "Views"

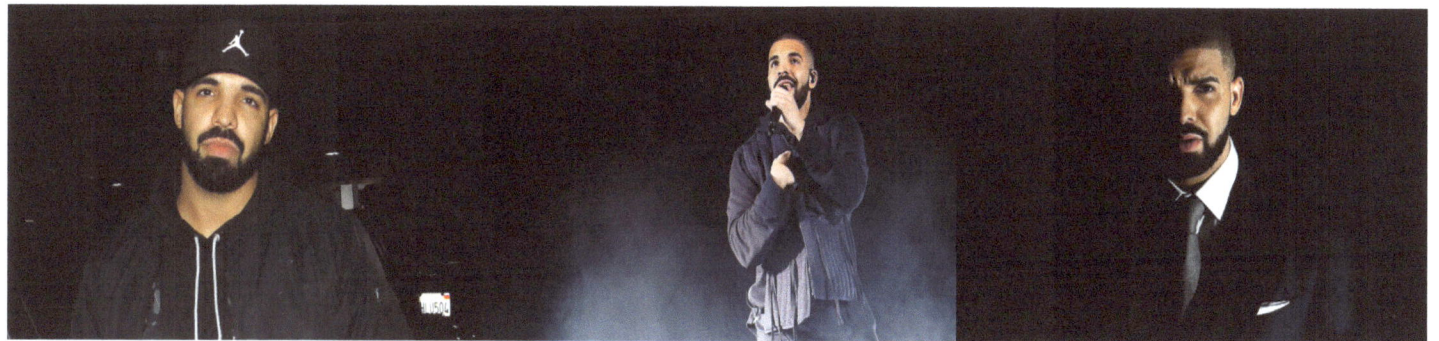

Drake is killing the charts right now with his 4th studio album "Views" which was released in 2016 by OVO Sound, Young Money Ent., Cash Money Records and Republic Records. He has 5 hits on this album alone: "Controlla", "One Dance", "Pop Style", "Too Good" & "Hotline Bling"! He has won a hand full of awards off of this album and from a few other singles he put out last year which includes; AMA for favorite rap/ hip hop album, BET Hip Hop Awards for best album of 2016, DMA International Album of the year and was also nominated for Best International Artist in the ARIA Music Awards. He originally wanted to name the album "Views from the six" but ended up changing it to "Views" so that it wouldn't lose its overall focus and could appeal to all areas and not just be concentrated on Toronto, Canada.

Drake delivers some great lyrical content which Intel's a calculated thought process; both characteristics make him stand out from his competition. He seems to be an artist that loves and thrives under pressure and his work ethic shows as he improves with every new track. If you haven't purchased the album yet then you should because this guy deserves it for all of his hard work!

- TAYVO BANK$

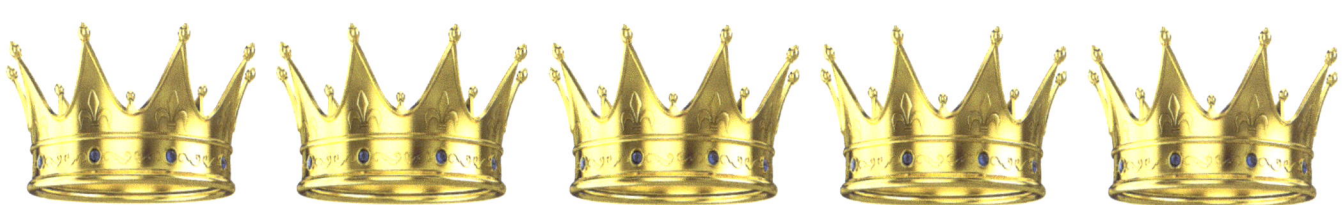

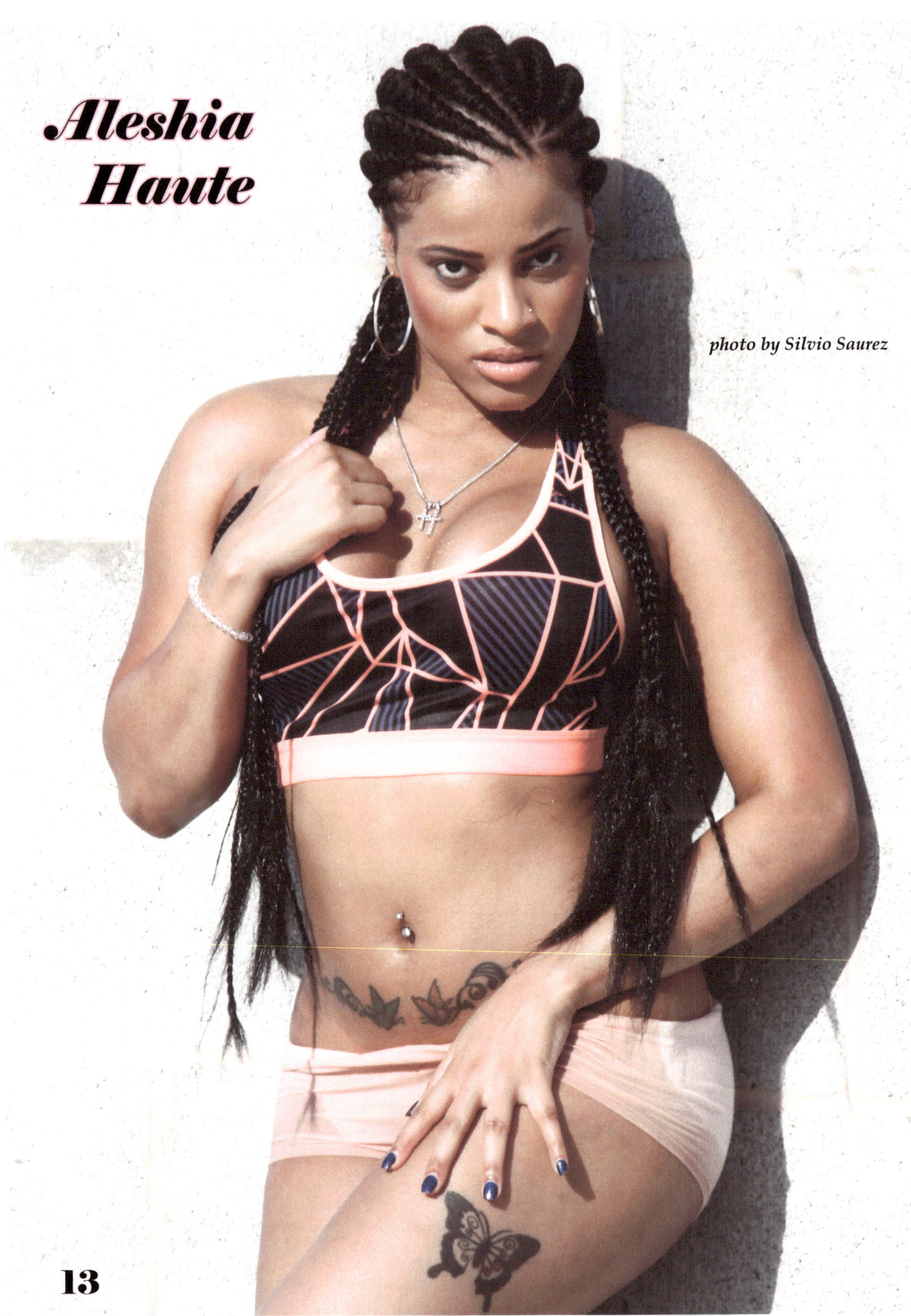

Aleshia Haute

photo by Silvio Saurez

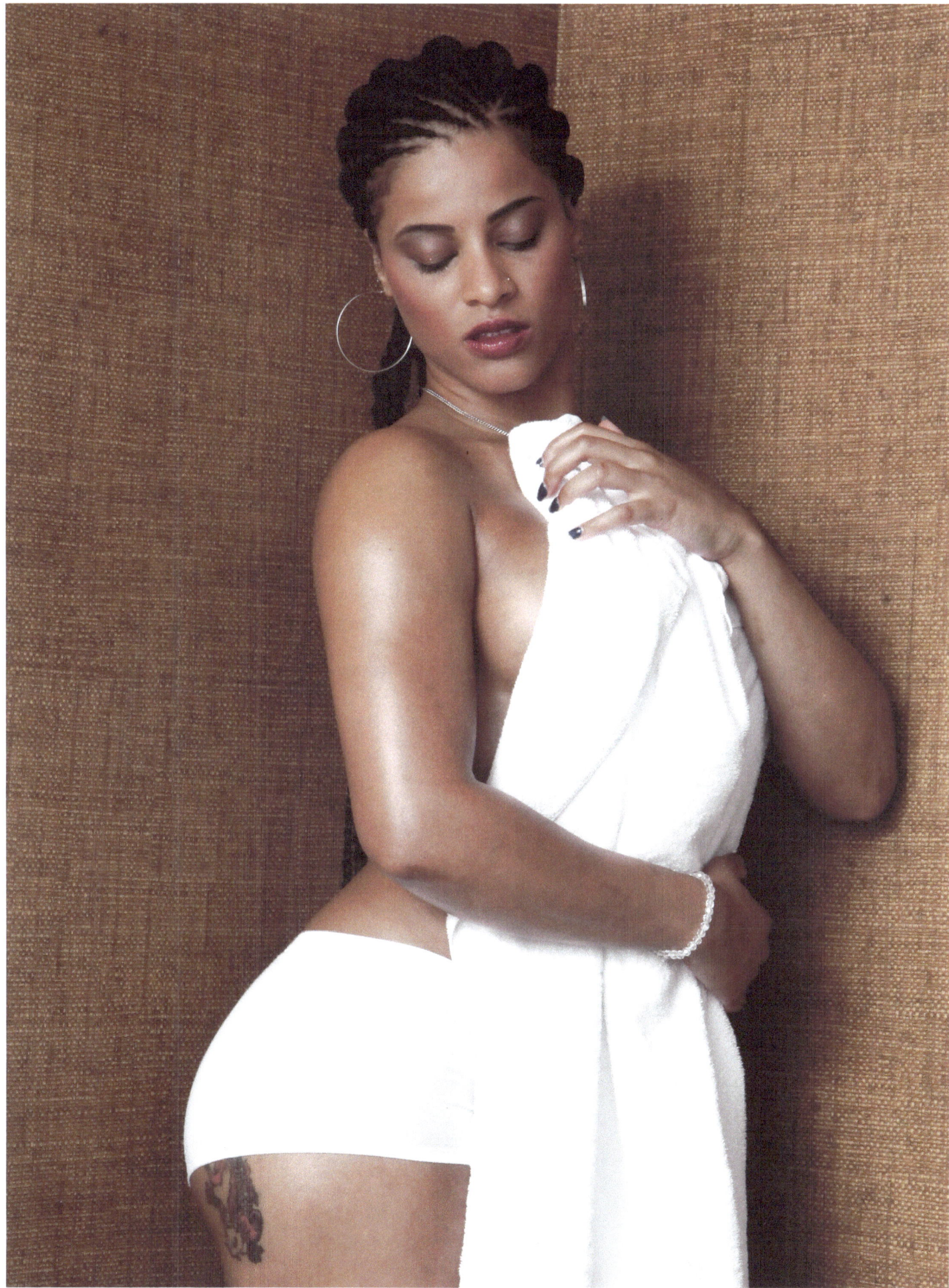

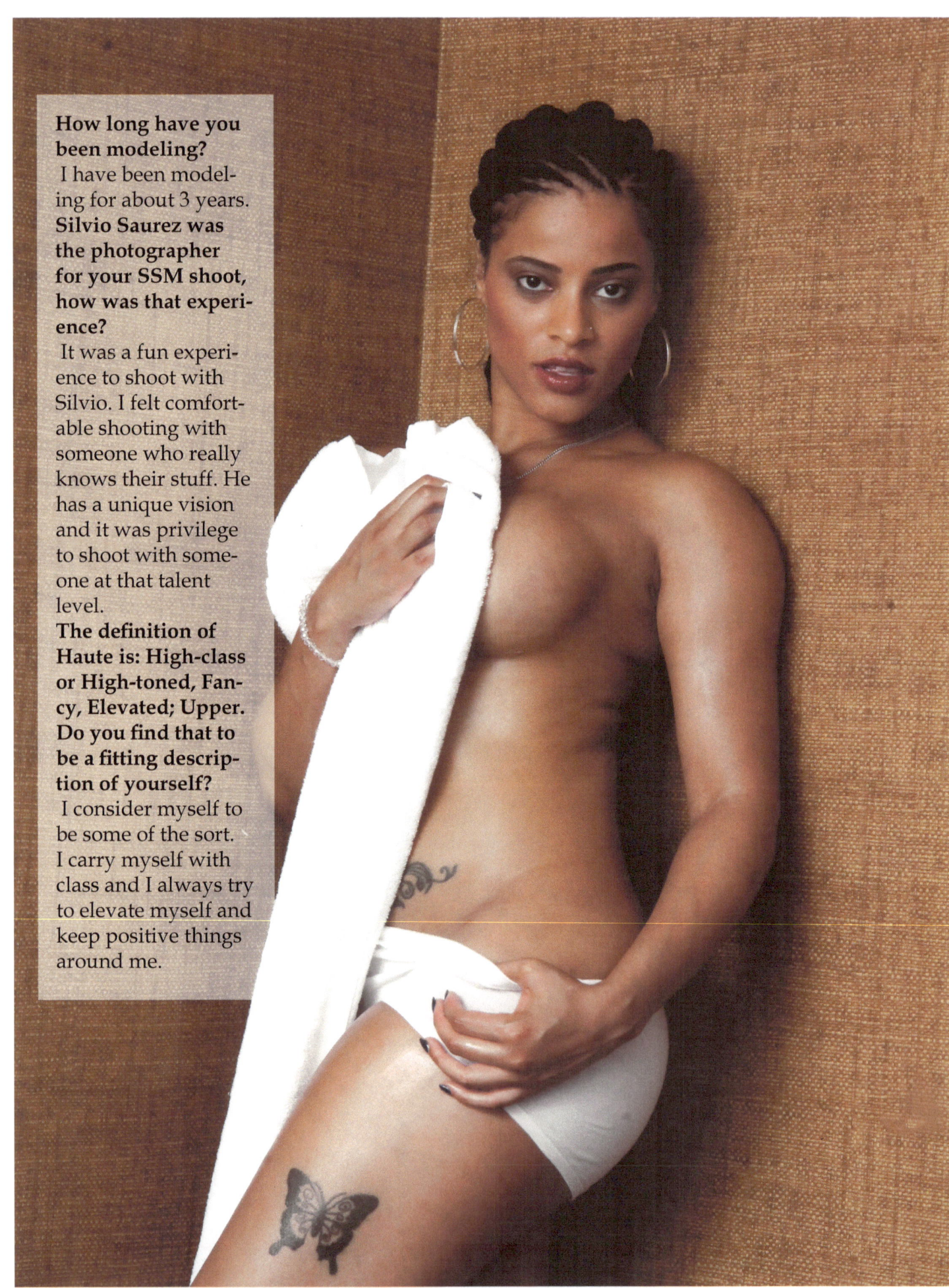

How long have you been modeling?
I have been modeling for about 3 years.

Silvio Saurez was the photographer for your SSM shoot, how was that experience?
It was a fun experience to shoot with Silvio. I felt comfortable shooting with someone who really knows their stuff. He has a unique vision and it was privilege to shoot with someone at that talent level.

The definition of Haute is: High-class or High-toned, Fancy, Elevated; Upper. Do you find that to be a fitting description of yourself?
I consider myself to be some of the sort. I carry myself with class and I always try to elevate myself and keep positive things around me.

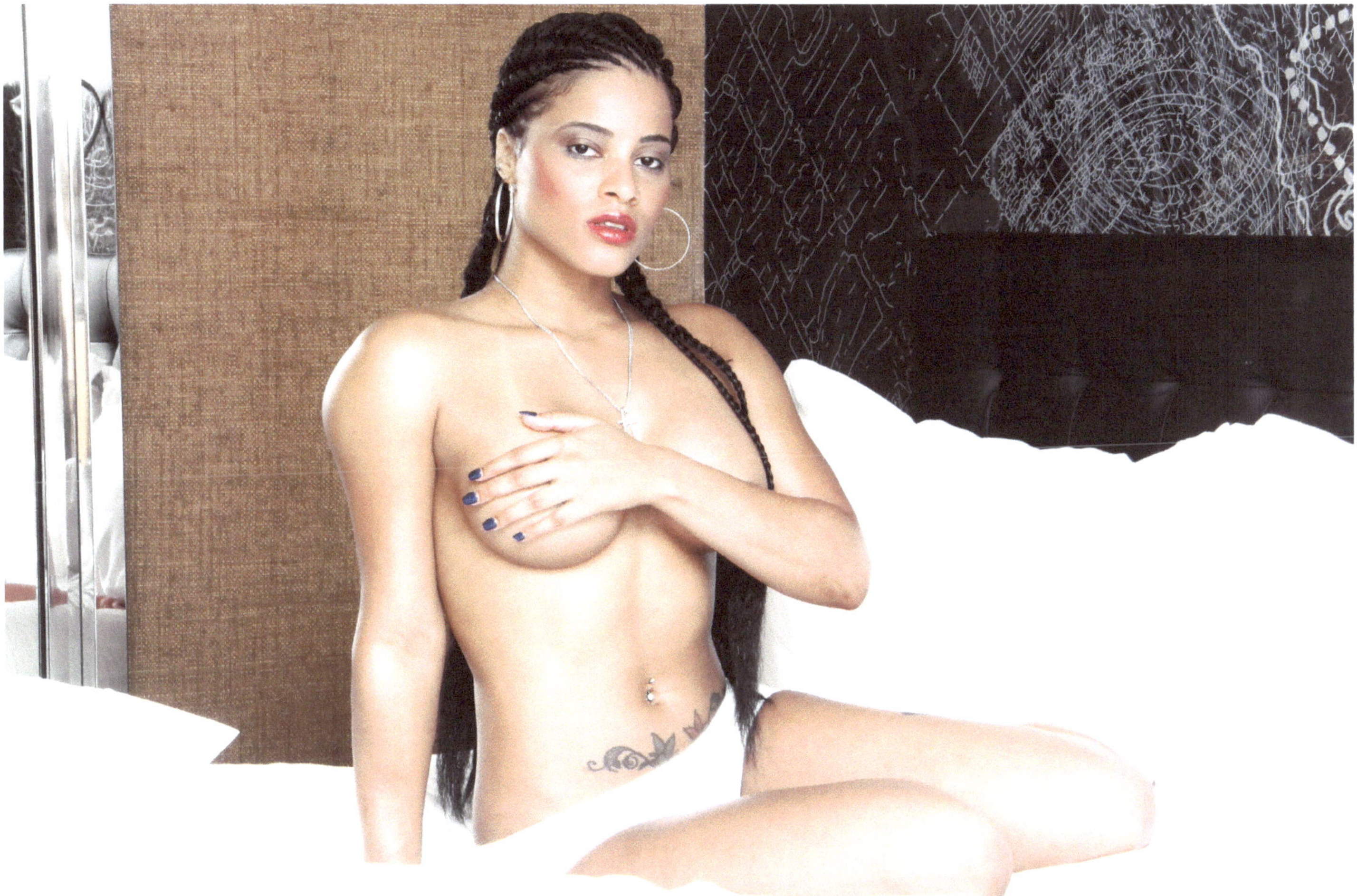

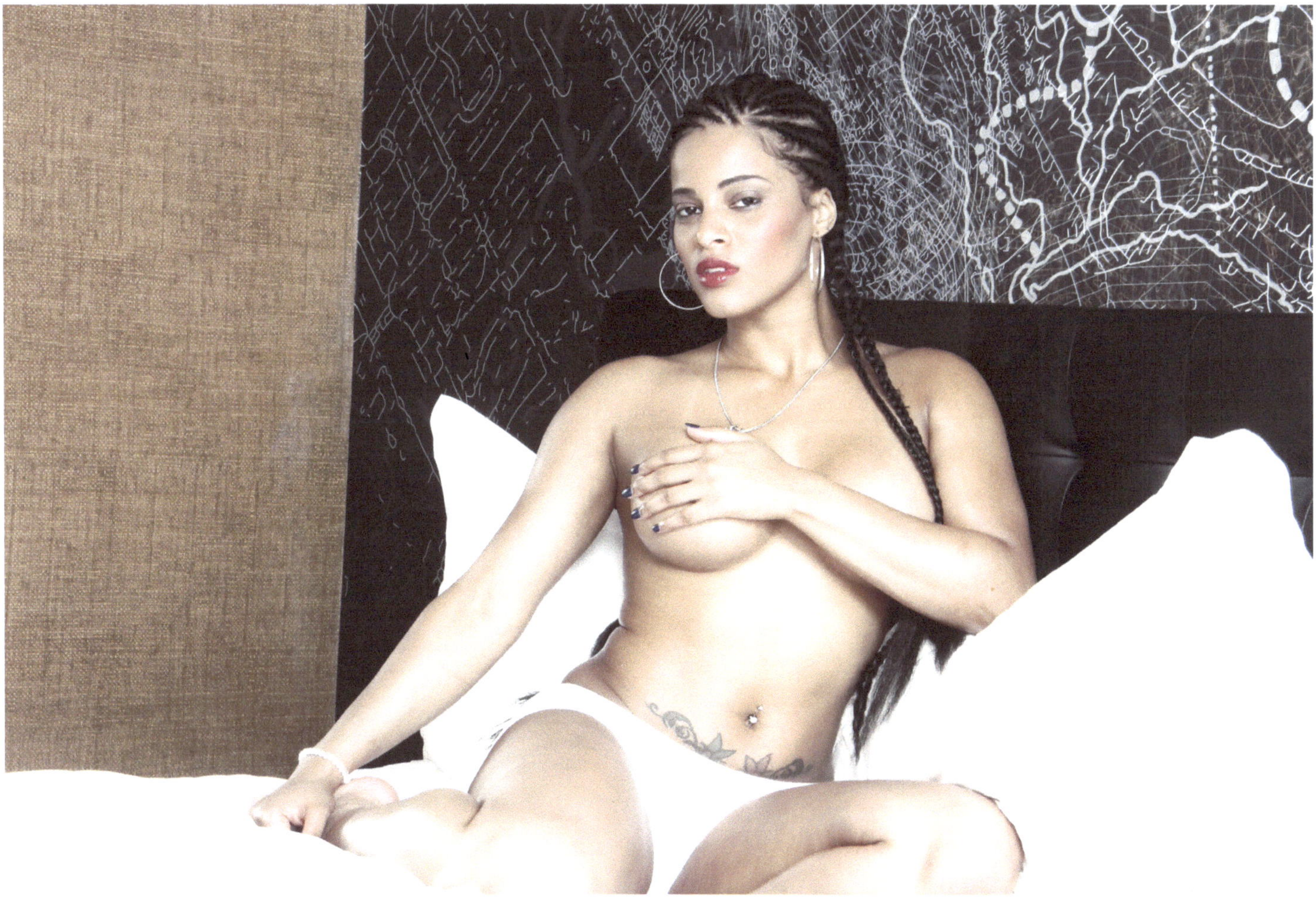

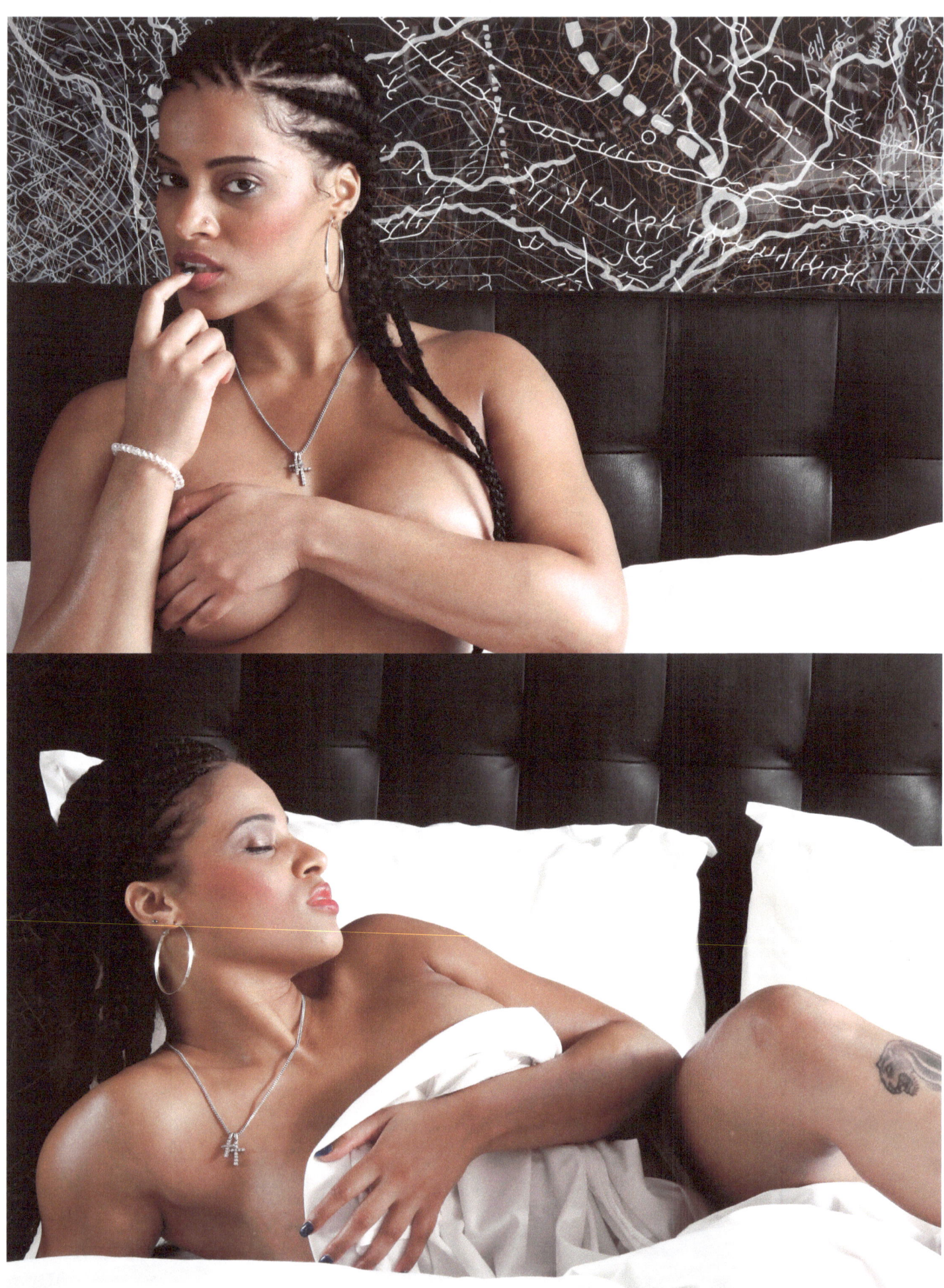

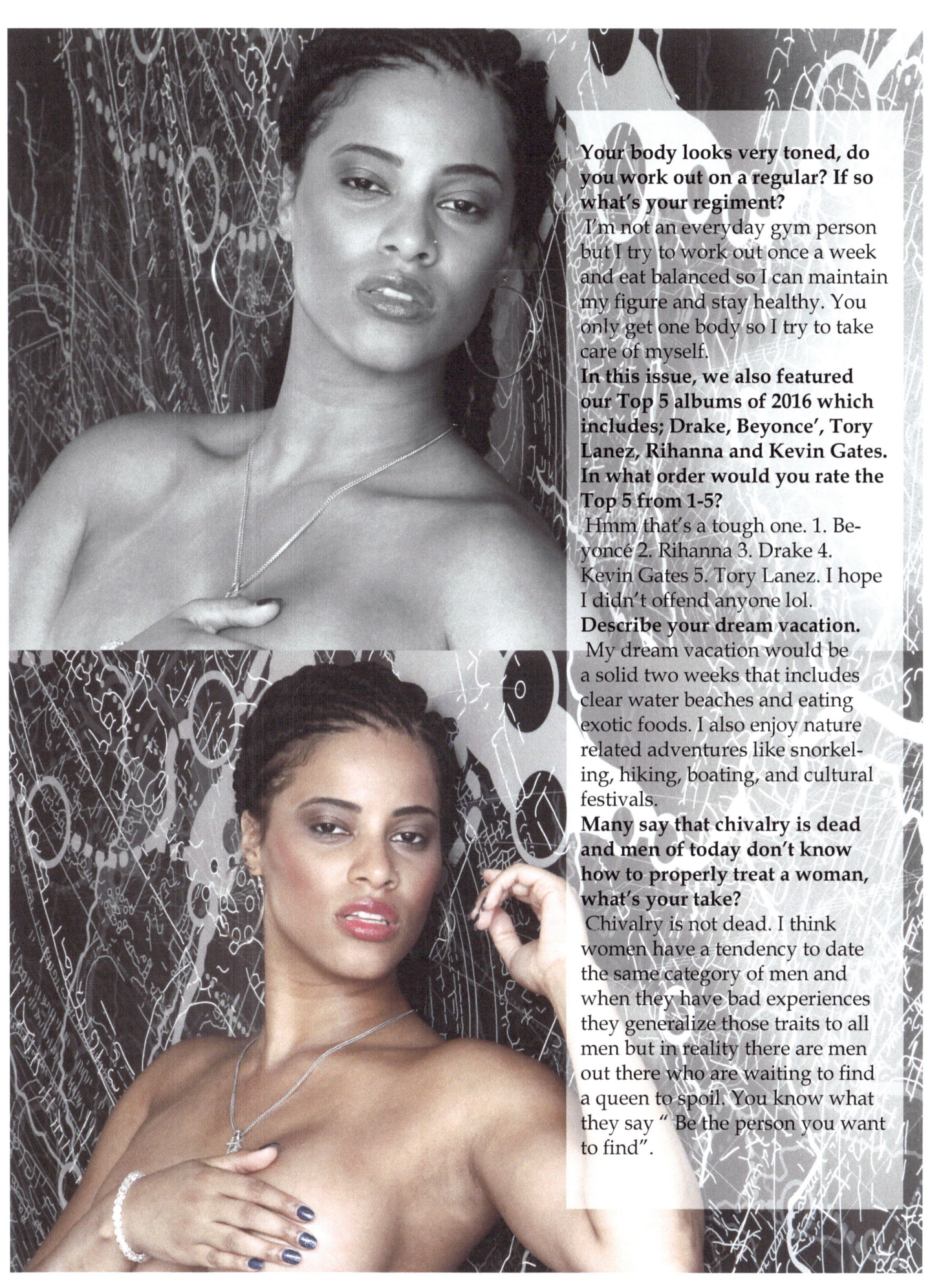

Your body looks very toned, do you work out on a regular? If so what's your regiment?
I'm not an everyday gym person but I try to work out once a week and eat balanced so I can maintain my figure and stay healthy. You only get one body so I try to take care of myself.

In this issue, we also featured our Top 5 albums of 2016 which includes; Drake, Beyonce', Tory Lanez, Rihanna and Kevin Gates. In what order would you rate the Top 5 from 1-5?
Hmm that's a tough one. 1. Beyoncé 2. Rihanna 3. Drake 4. Kevin Gates 5. Tory Lanez. I hope I didn't offend anyone lol.

Describe your dream vacation.
My dream vacation would be a solid two weeks that includes clear water beaches and eating exotic foods. I also enjoy nature related adventures like snorkeling, hiking, boating, and cultural festivals.

Many say that chivalry is dead and men of today don't know how to properly treat a woman, what's your take?
Chivalry is not dead. I think women have a tendency to date the same category of men and when they have bad experiences they generalize those traits to all men but in reality there are men out there who are waiting to find a queen to spoil. You know what they say " Be the person you want to find".

Beyoncé - Lemonade

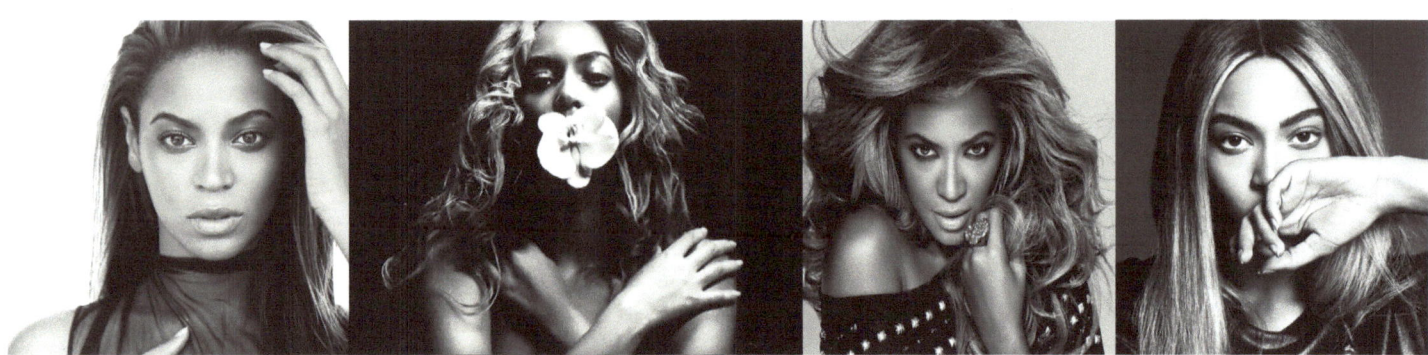

Beyoncé, now only 35 still has the game on lock! She sold around 485,000 copies of her 2016 release "Lemonade" within the first week. "Lemonade" which is her 6th studio album was released by her label Parkwood Ent. and distributed by Columbia Records. This album included music from several different genres: R&B, Reggae, Gospel, Trap, Rock, etc. She also has a few artist features that includes; Jack White, James Blake, The Weeknd & the very talented Kendrick Lamar. Almost half of the album consisted of hit singles with "Formation" & "Sorry" bringing the most heat.

Beyoncé a multi-platinum artist is also an awesome role model for all ages and genders because she keeps it real! Even though some people dislike her realness, most people love that about her. It was a great decision to embark on a solo career after the success of Destiny's Child and she has proven that within her every breathing moment. If you're not a fan yet and you love music, you should definitely cop this album just to intimately experience her talent as a soulful artist.

- TAYVO BANK$

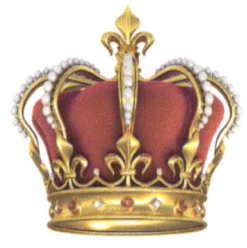 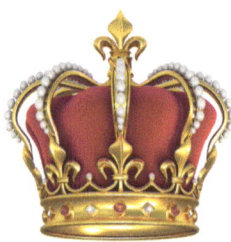 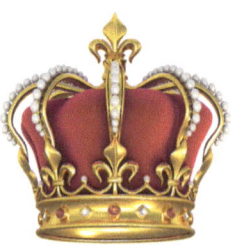 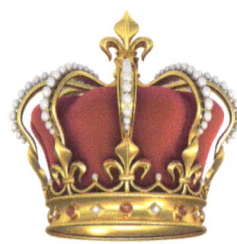 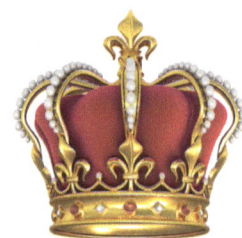

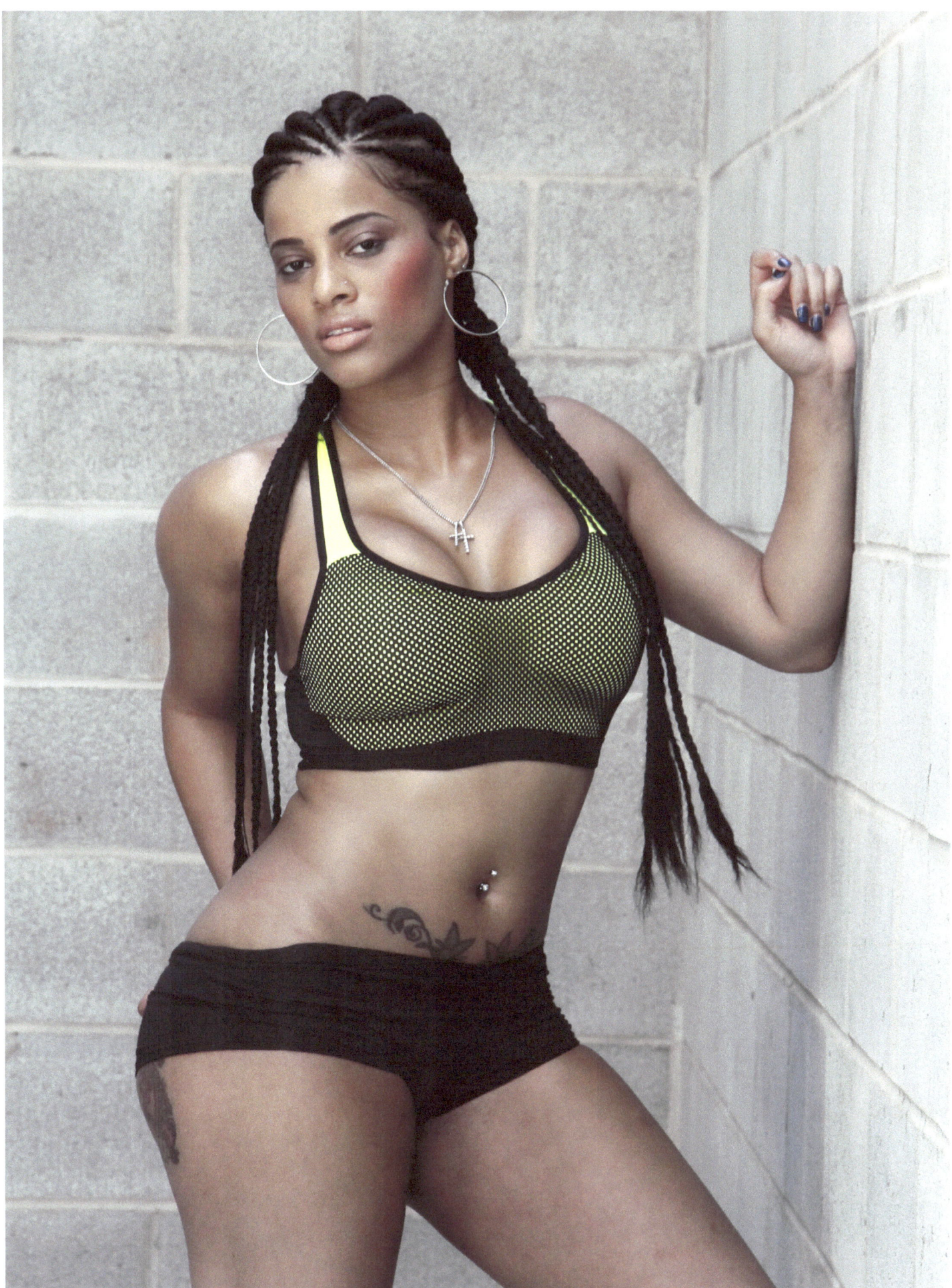

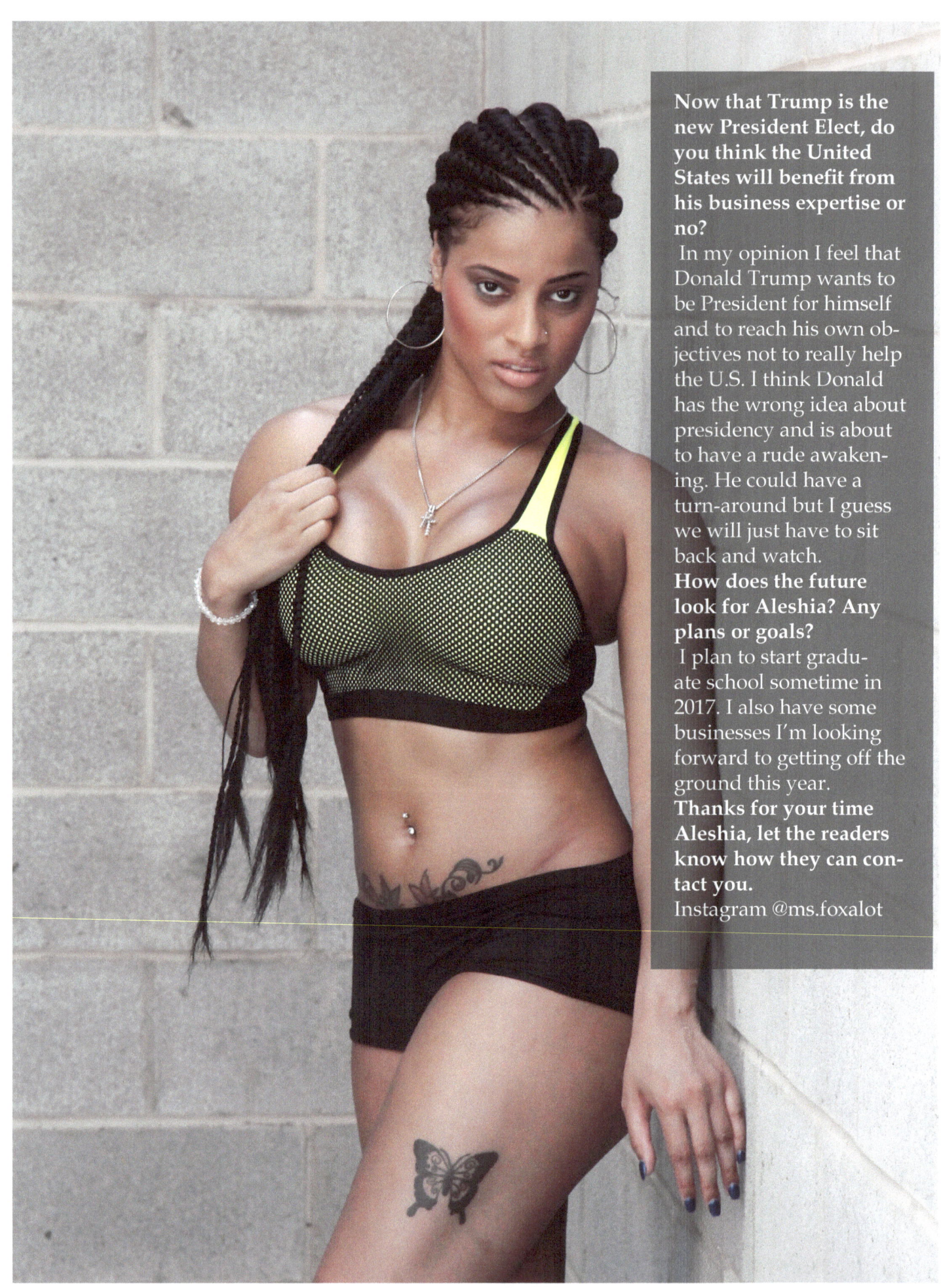

Now that Trump is the new President Elect, do you think the United States will benefit from his business expertise or no?
In my opinion I feel that Donald Trump wants to be President for himself and to reach his own objectives not to really help the U.S. I think Donald has the wrong idea about presidency and is about to have a rude awakening. He could have a turn-around but I guess we will just have to sit back and watch.

How does the future look for Aleshia? Any plans or goals?
I plan to start graduate school sometime in 2017. I also have some businesses I'm looking forward to getting off the ground this year.

Thanks for your time Aleshia, let the readers know how they can contact you.
Instagram @ms.foxalot

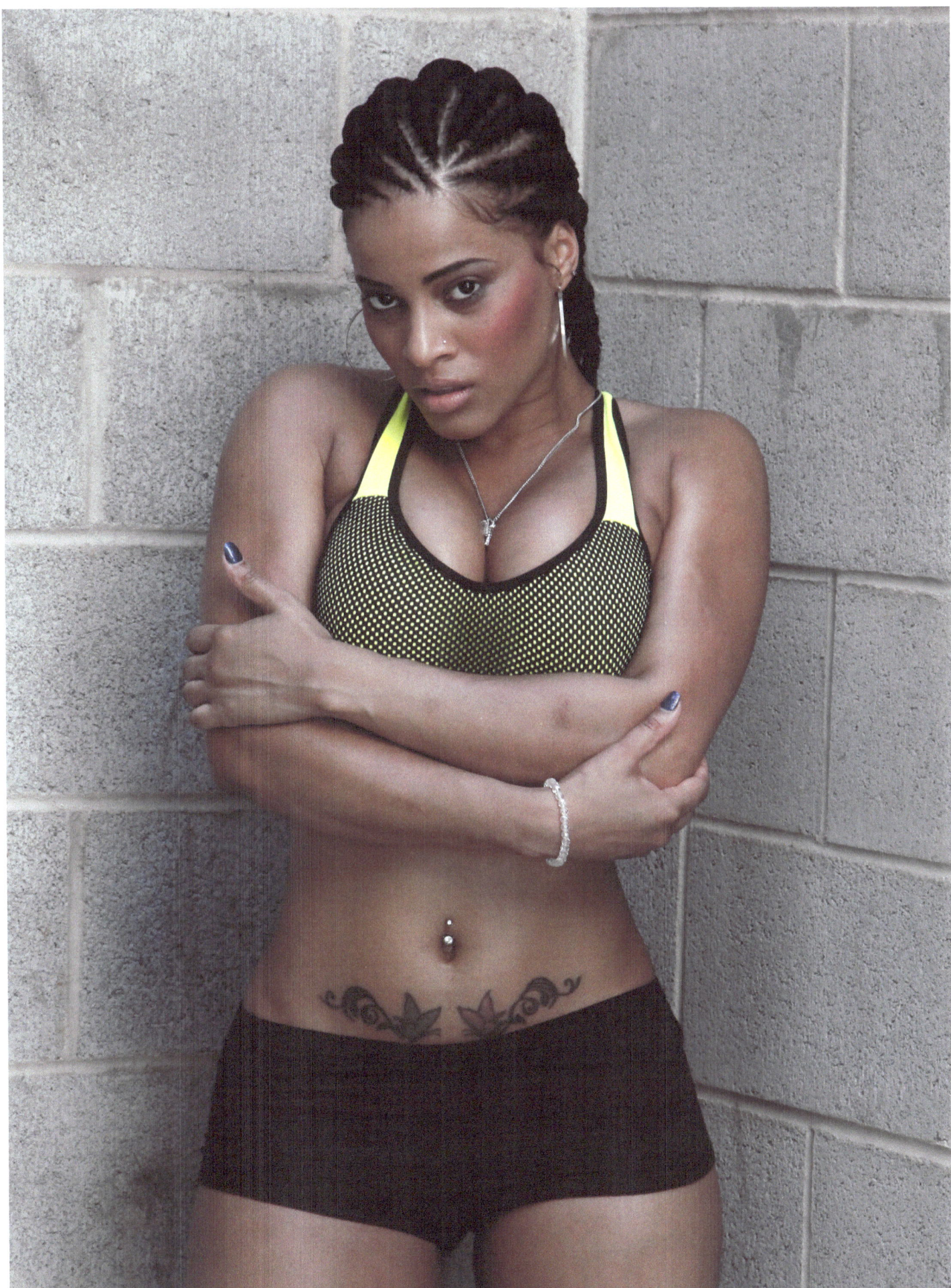

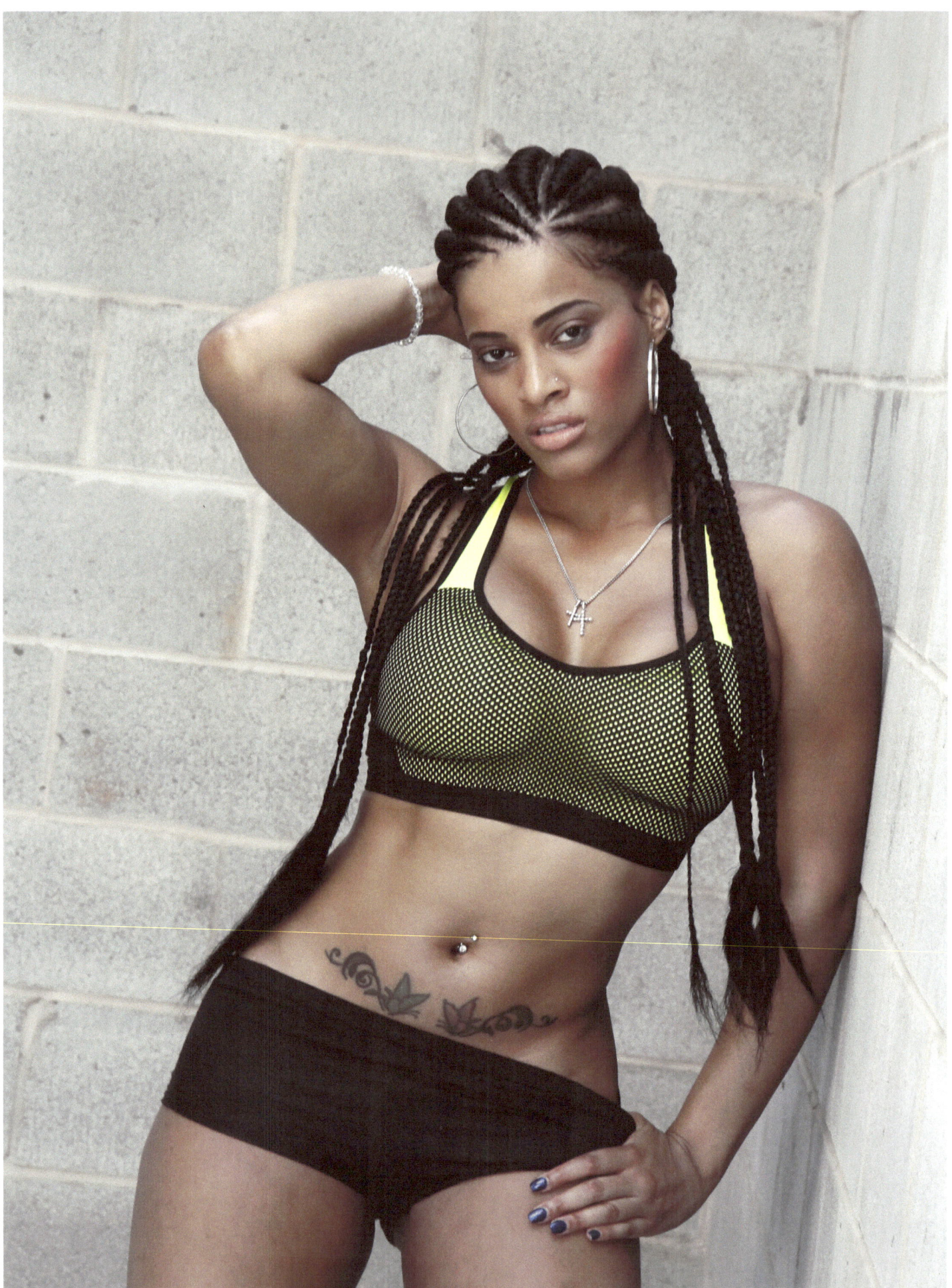

Kevin Gates - Islah

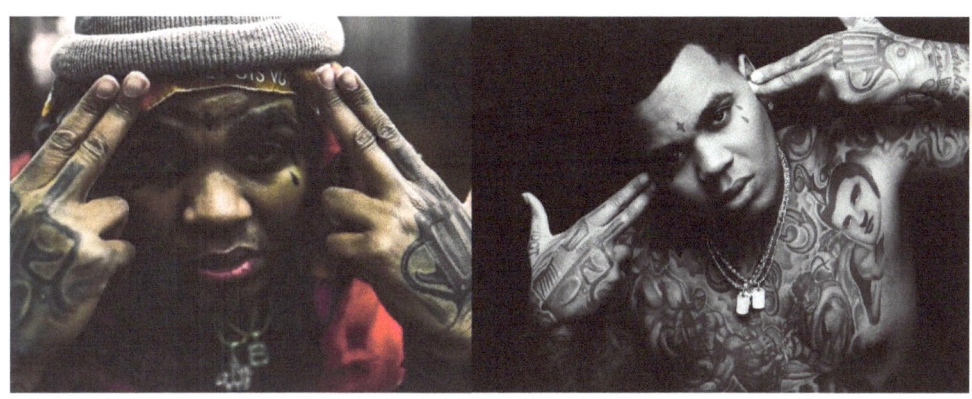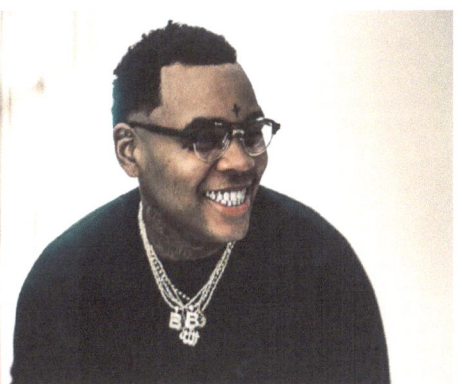

Kevin Gates is one of the most popular Artist out right now, who's actually been in the game since 2006. He came into the industry with a unique flow that the fans love and resonate with. Gates dropped his debut album "Islah" in 2016 which was released by Independent Label, Bread Winners Association and Atlantic Records. This album has 6 hit singles; "Kno One", "La Famalia", "The Truth", "Really Really", "Time for That" & his hottest one yet; "2 Phones".

Kevin Gates named this album after his daughter Islah. You can tell he puts his heart and soul into his work. The album is also very diverse; he raps, sings and also tells stories in each song. Go get this album to hear all of his real life stories and forget about what gossip feeds you!

- TAYVO BANK$

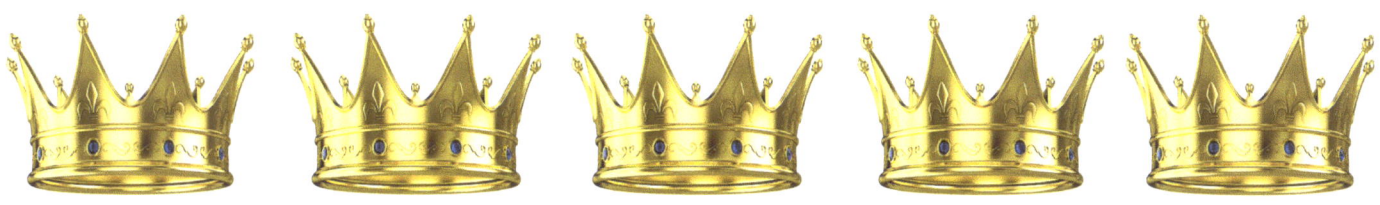

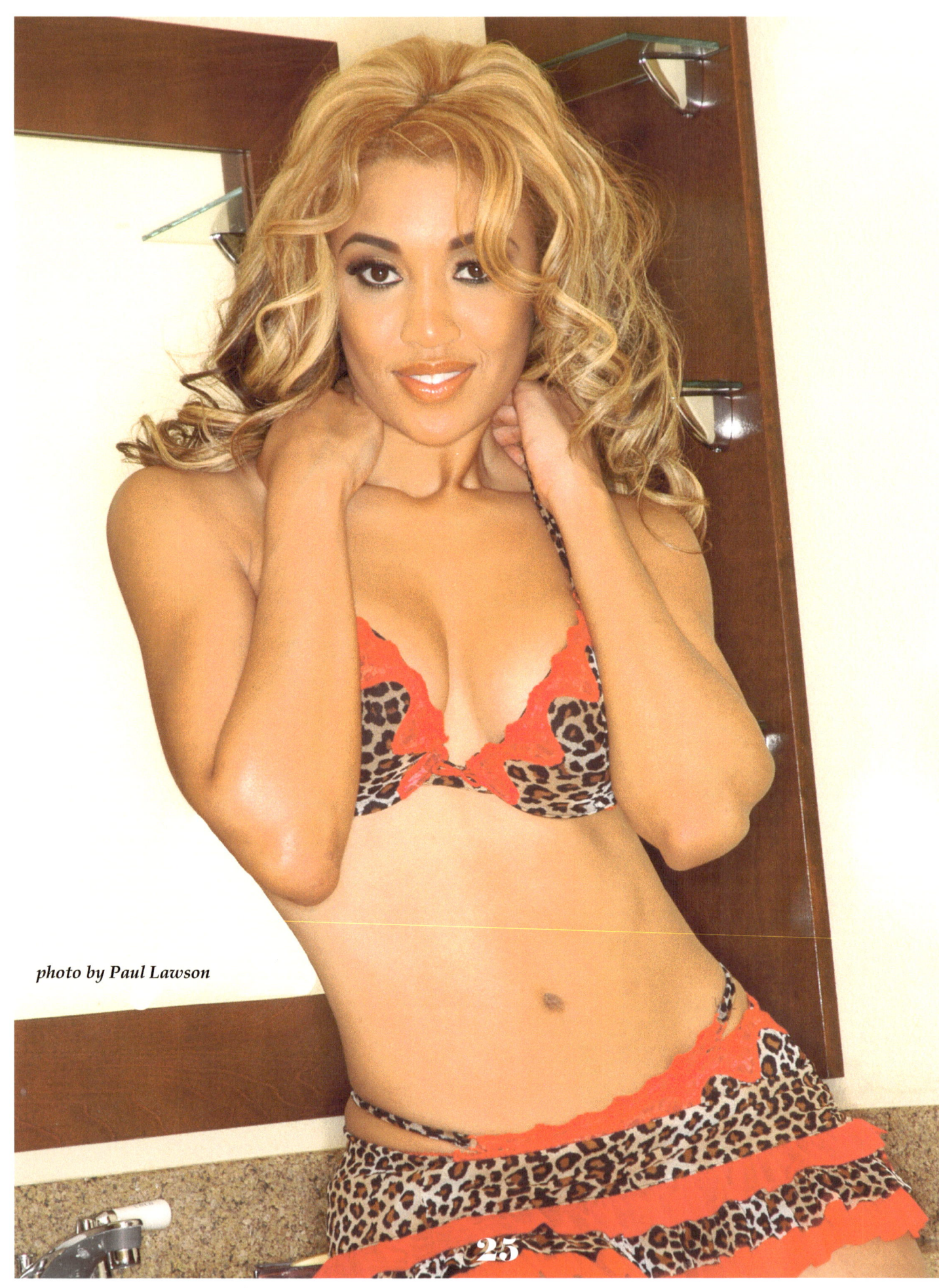

photo by Paul Lawson

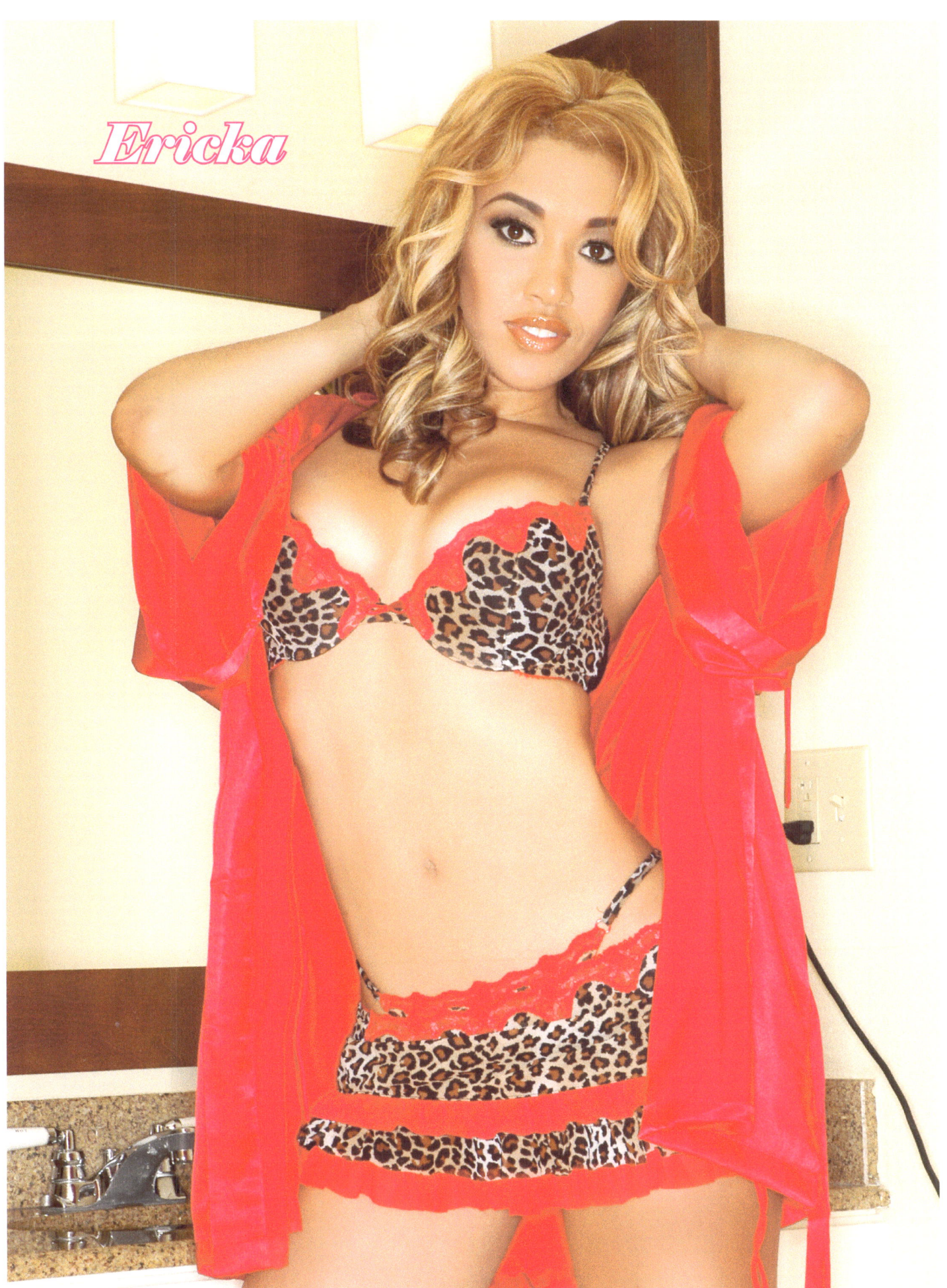

Ericka

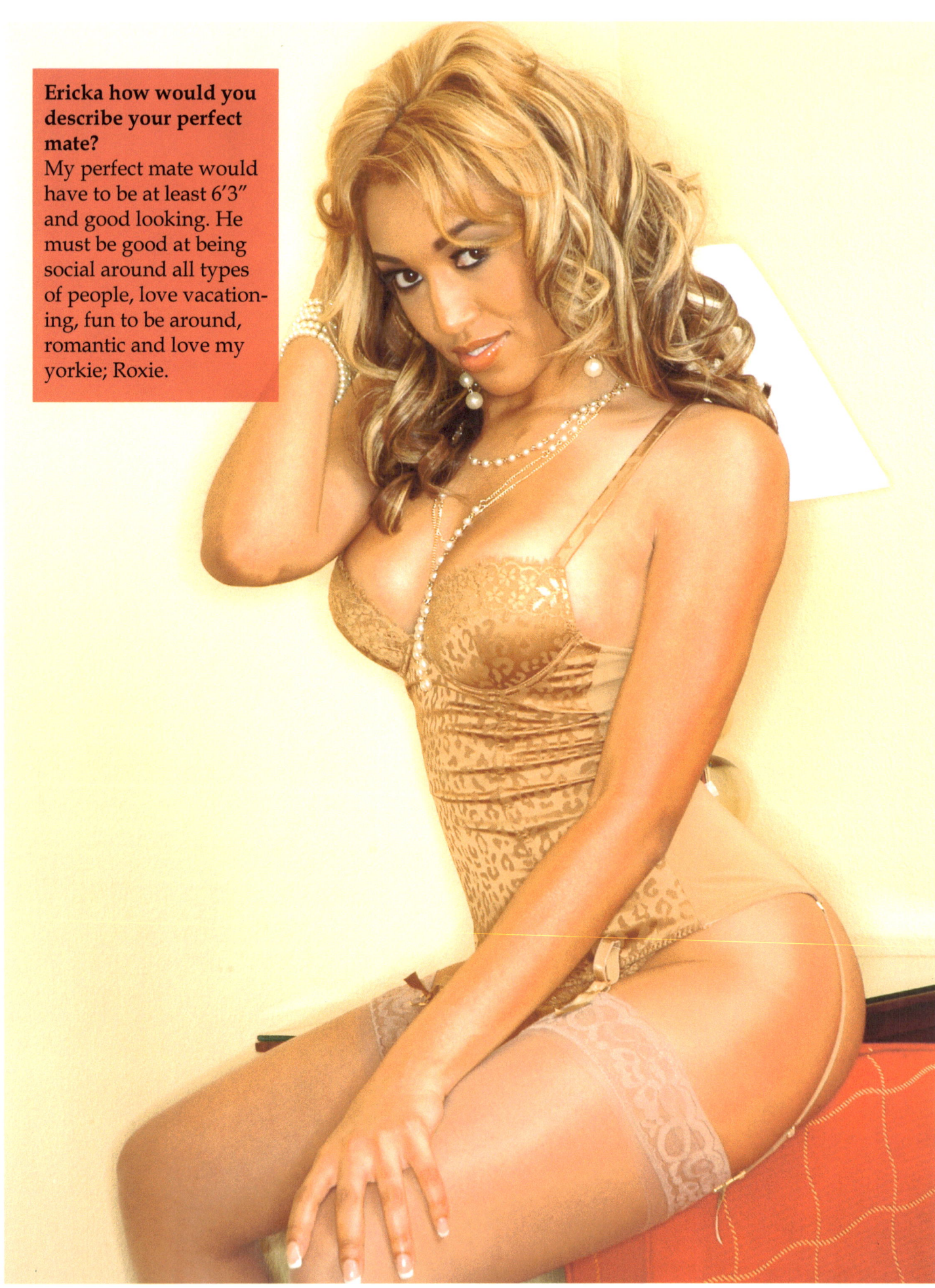

Ericka how would you describe your perfect mate?
My perfect mate would have to be at least 6'3" and good looking. He must be good at being social around all types of people, love vacationing, fun to be around, romantic and love my yorkie; Roxie.

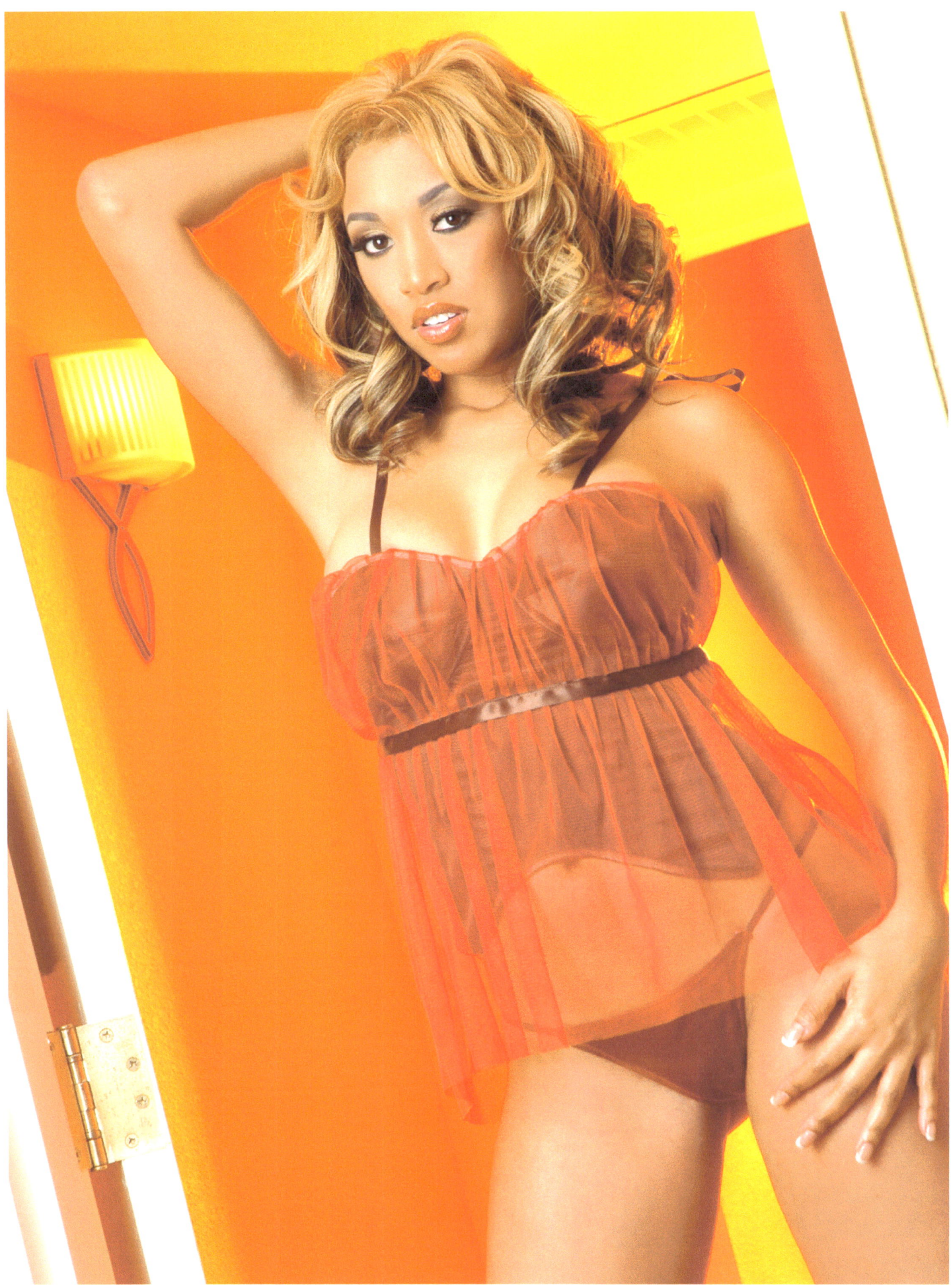

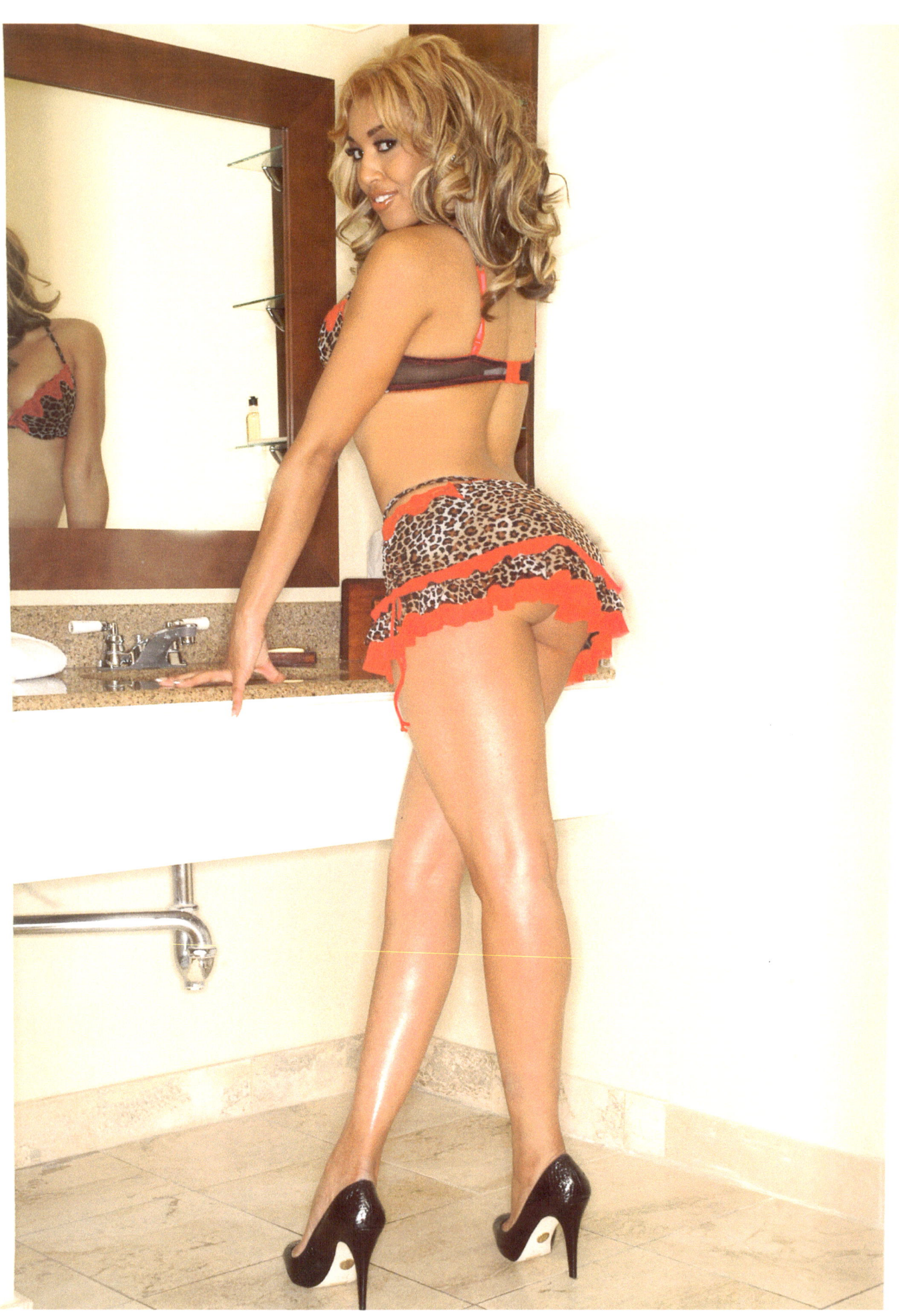

Tory Lanez - I Told You

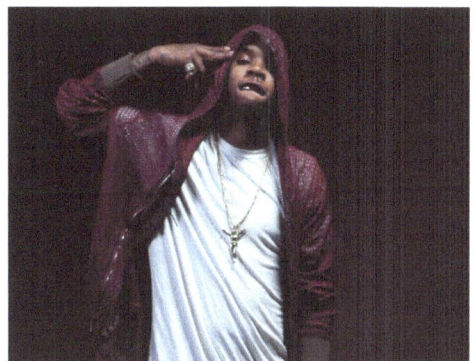 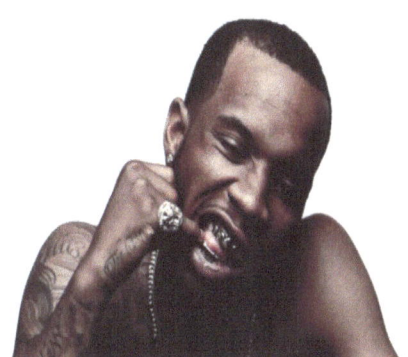 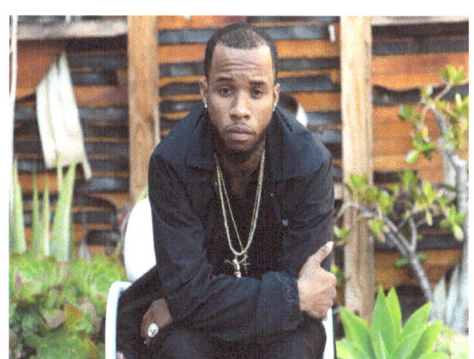

Tory Lanez is a hot R&B and Rap artist who's working his way to the top! His newest album "I Told You" is fire, especially with the ladies. This album was released in 2016 by Mad love & Interscope Records features two hits "Say It" & "Luv".

Tory a native of Toronto, Canada got a buzz when he released a hot mixtape called "Lost Cause", ever since it dropped his audience has been begging him to release more and more tracks. Lanez is one of the realest artists that I've ever heard. So if you haven't been paying attention to the new music that blessed the industry in 2016 you definitely need to tune in and cop Tory Lanez album you won't regret it!

- TAYVO BANK$

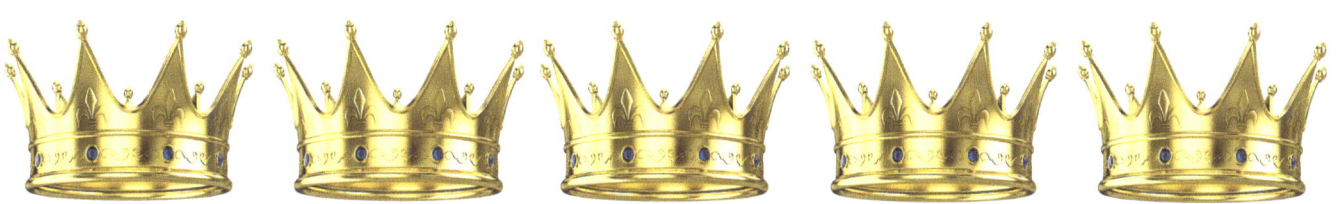

Chivon

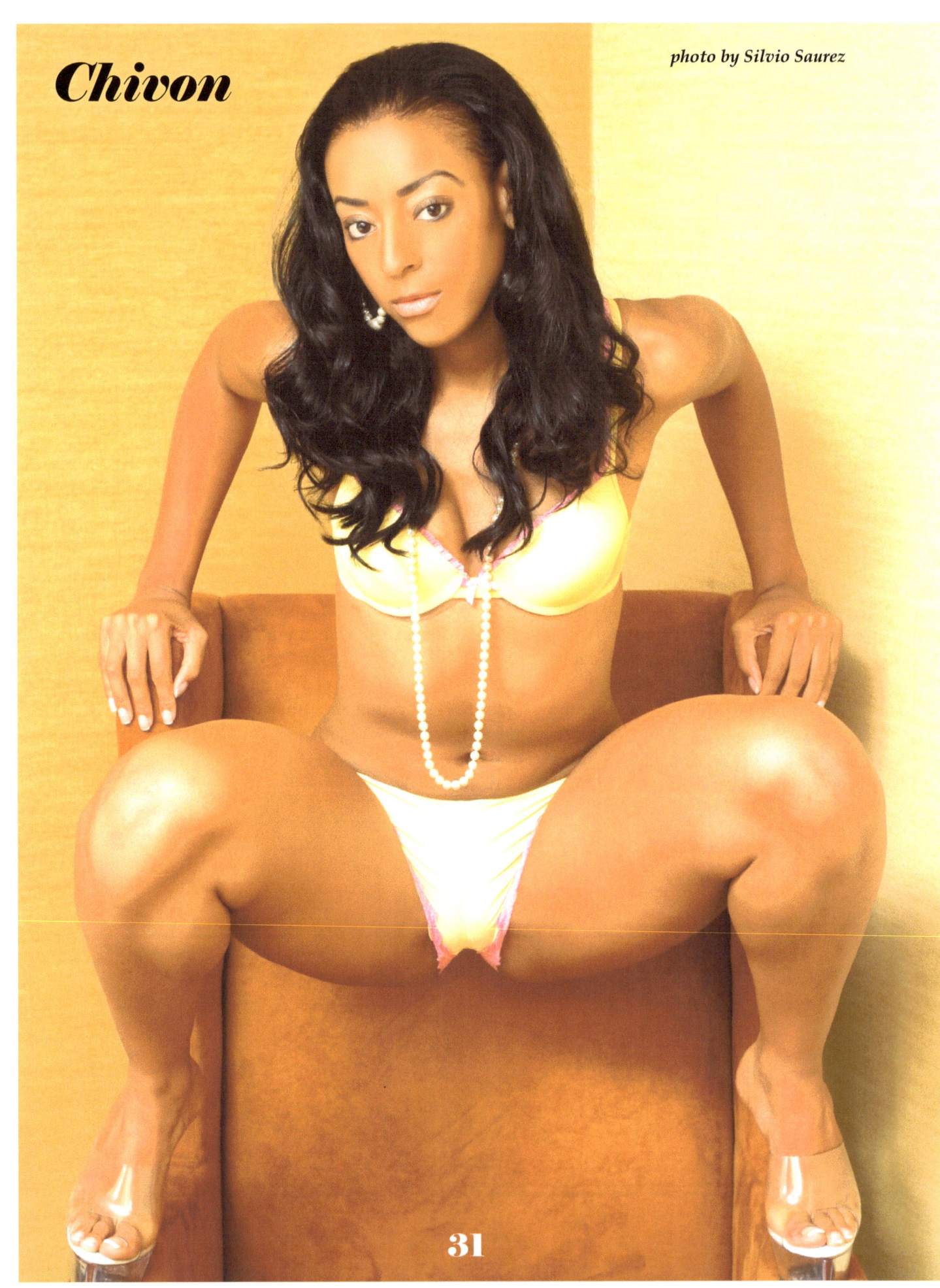

31

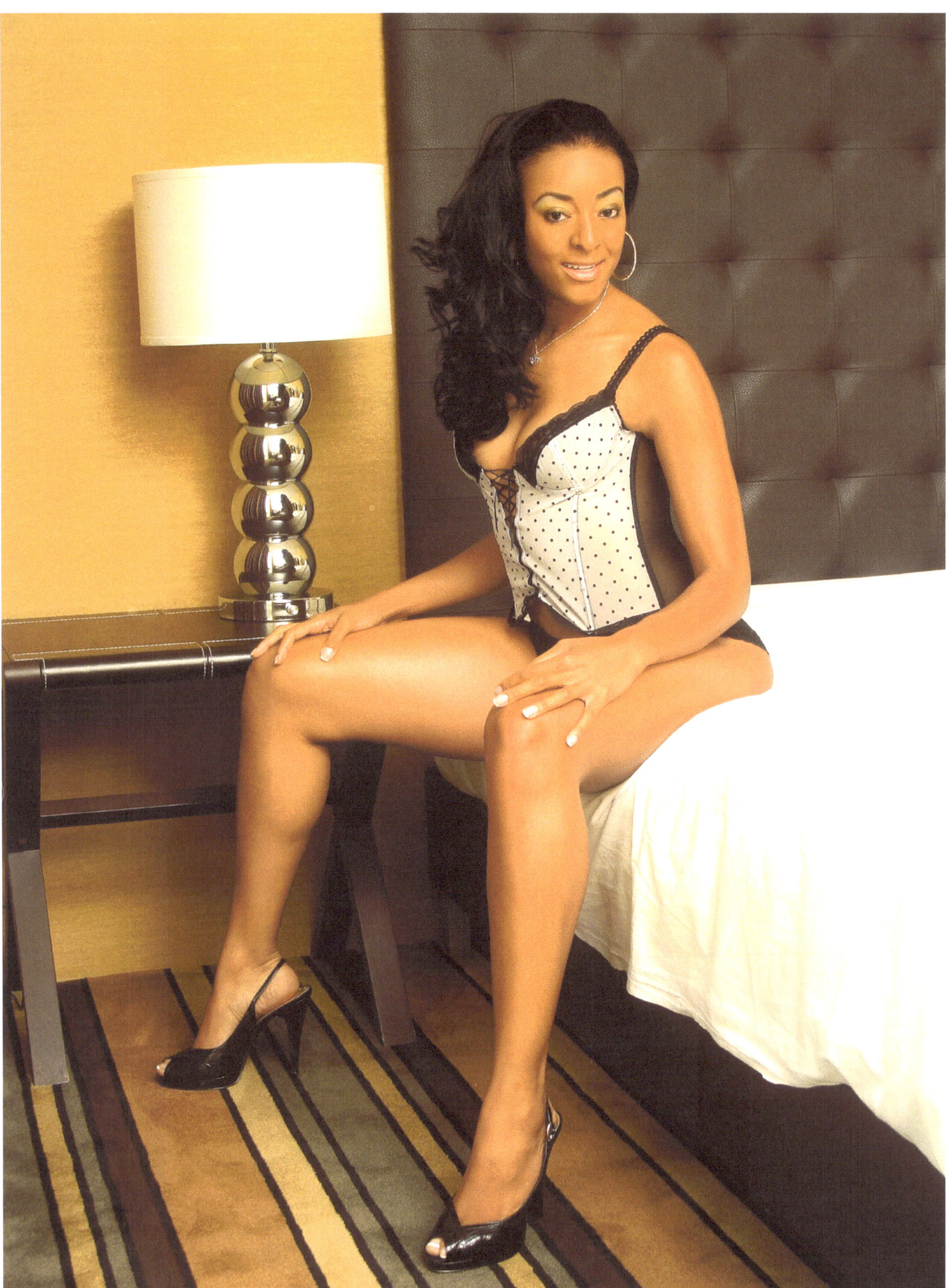

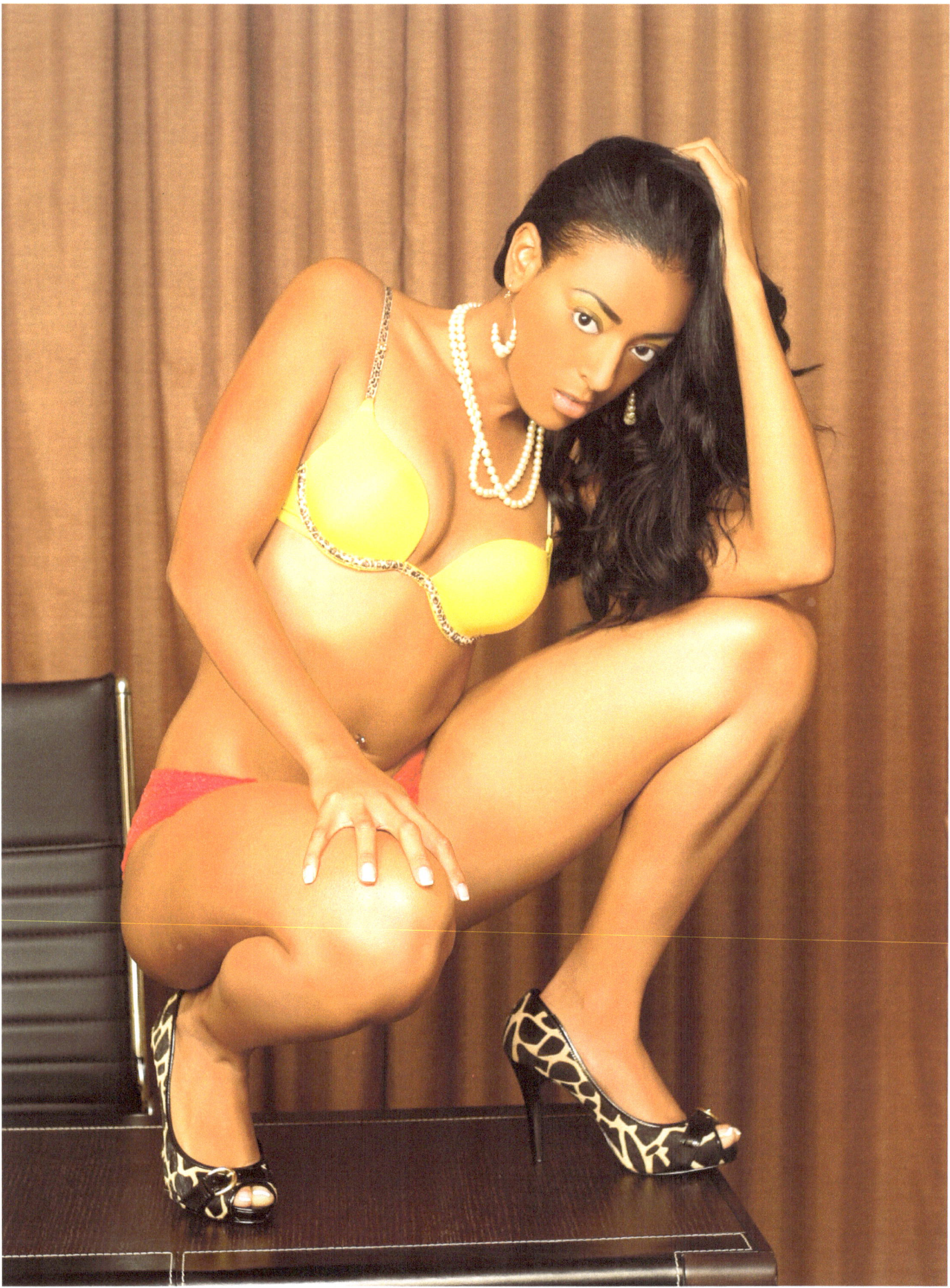

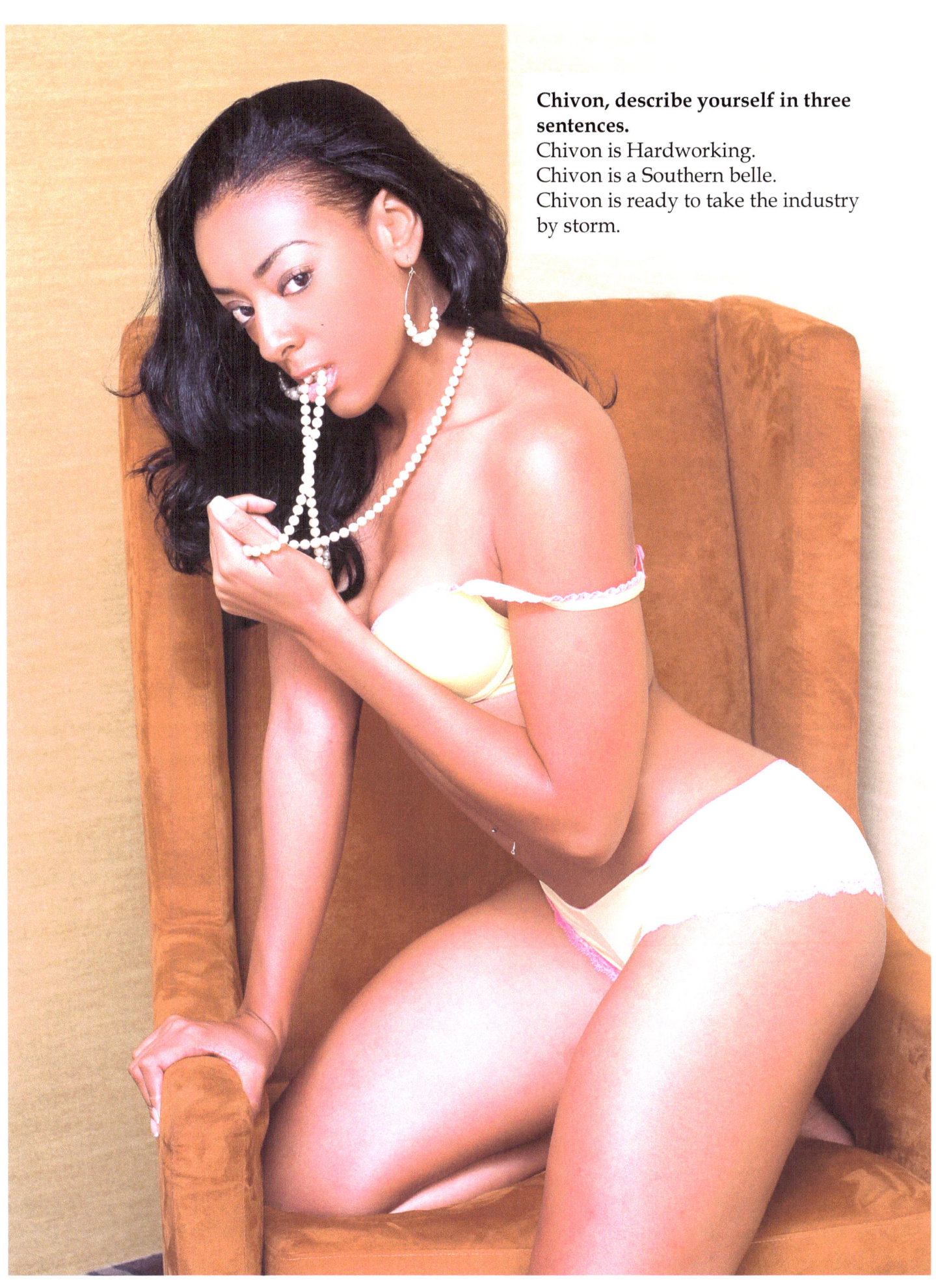

Chivon, describe yourself in three sentences.
Chivon is Hardworking.
Chivon is a Southern belle.
Chivon is ready to take the industry by storm.

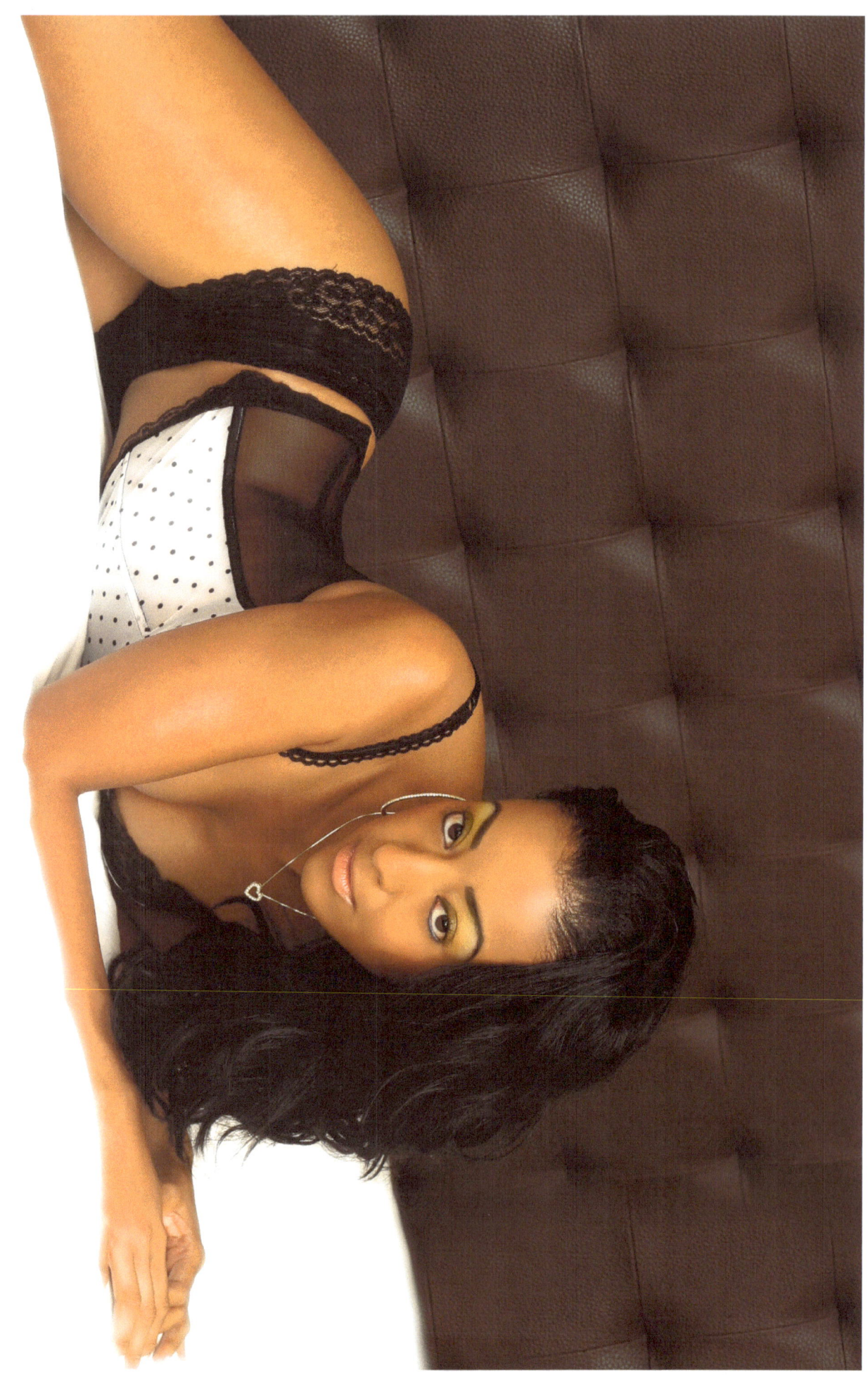

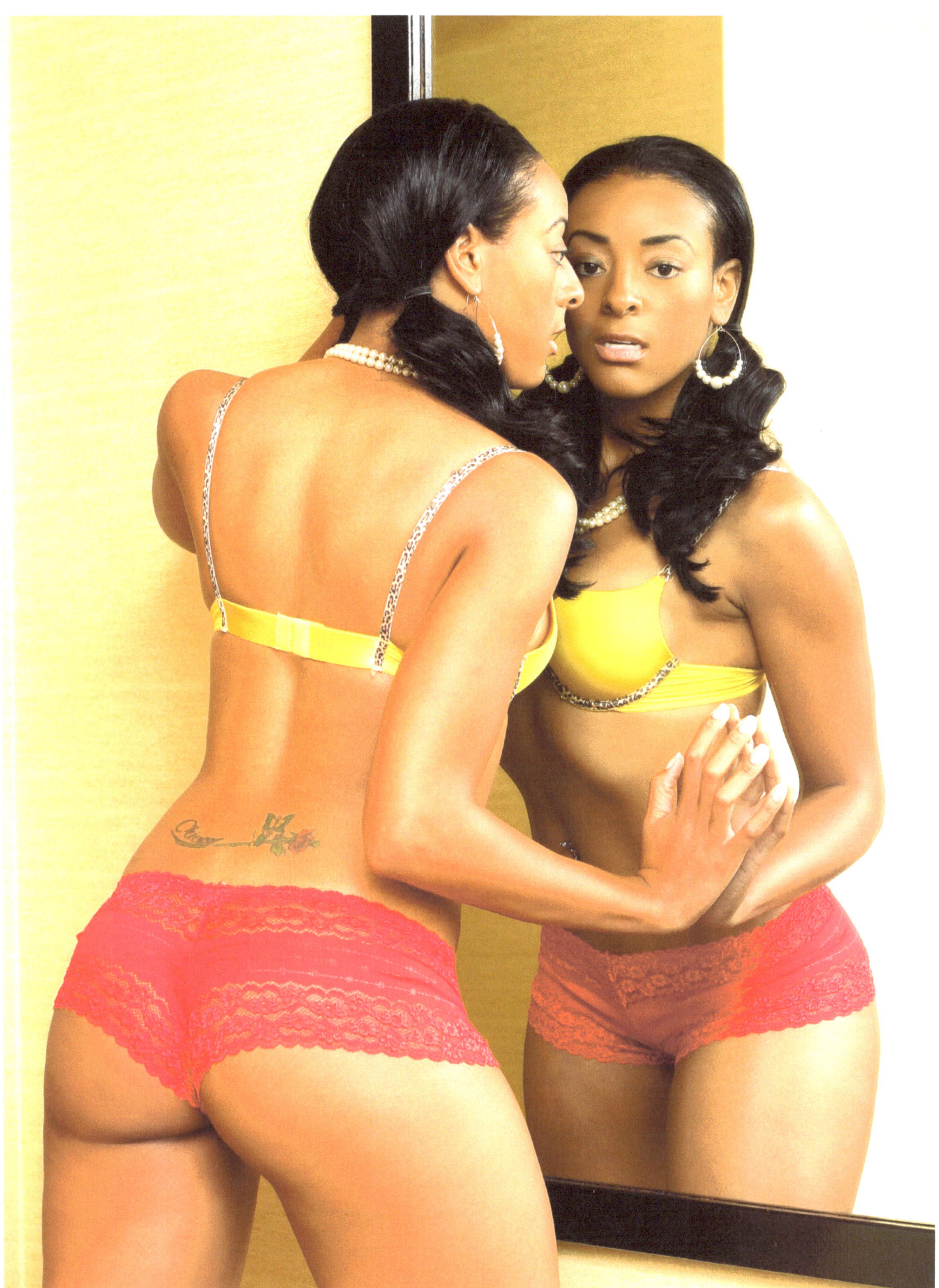

Rihanna - Anti

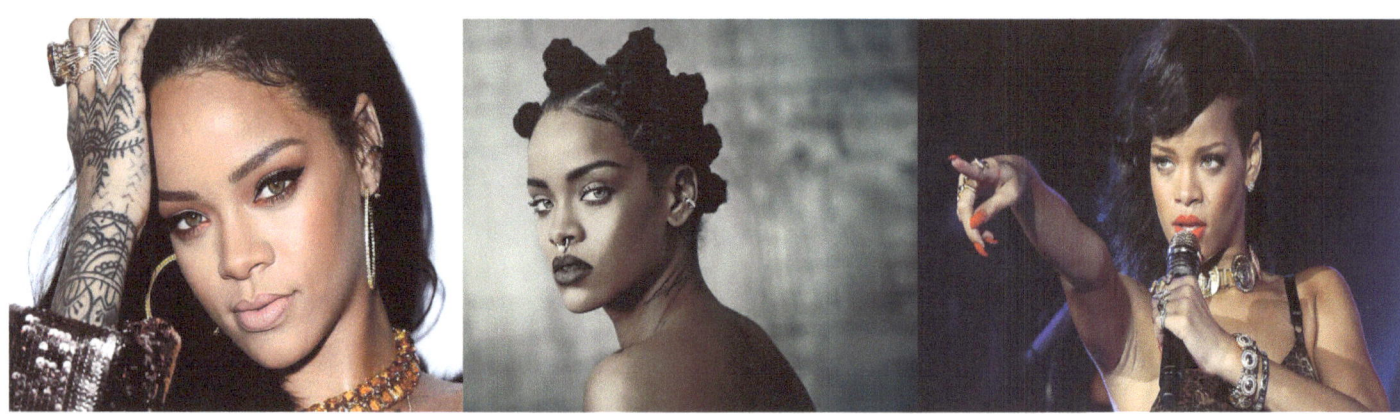

Rihanna is a very talented young lady who has the innate ability to captivate her audience. Her 2016 album "Anti" was released by Westbury Road and Roc Nation in January. This album was a major hit and she even changed her genres to R&B and Pop from the normal Dance and Club style, like she previously released. It definitely still worked for her though and the audience loved it as sales pushed "Anti" to Platinum status in only 2 days.

Rihanna has a plethora of hits on this album; "Work", "Kiss it Better", "Desperado" & "Needed Me", portrays some of her best work. She also got nominated for top R&B album at the BMA's. This woman is brilliant when it comes to entertaining and making hits. You would swear that she just stayed in the studio all day recording songs back to back. This album is a must have!

- TAYVO BANK$

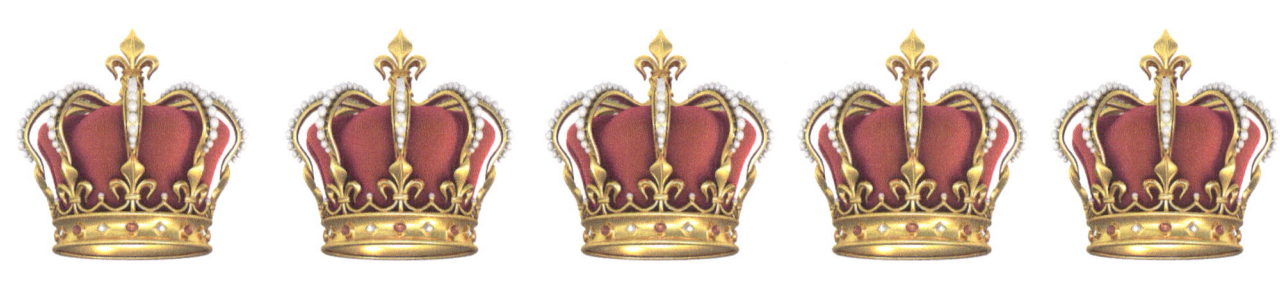

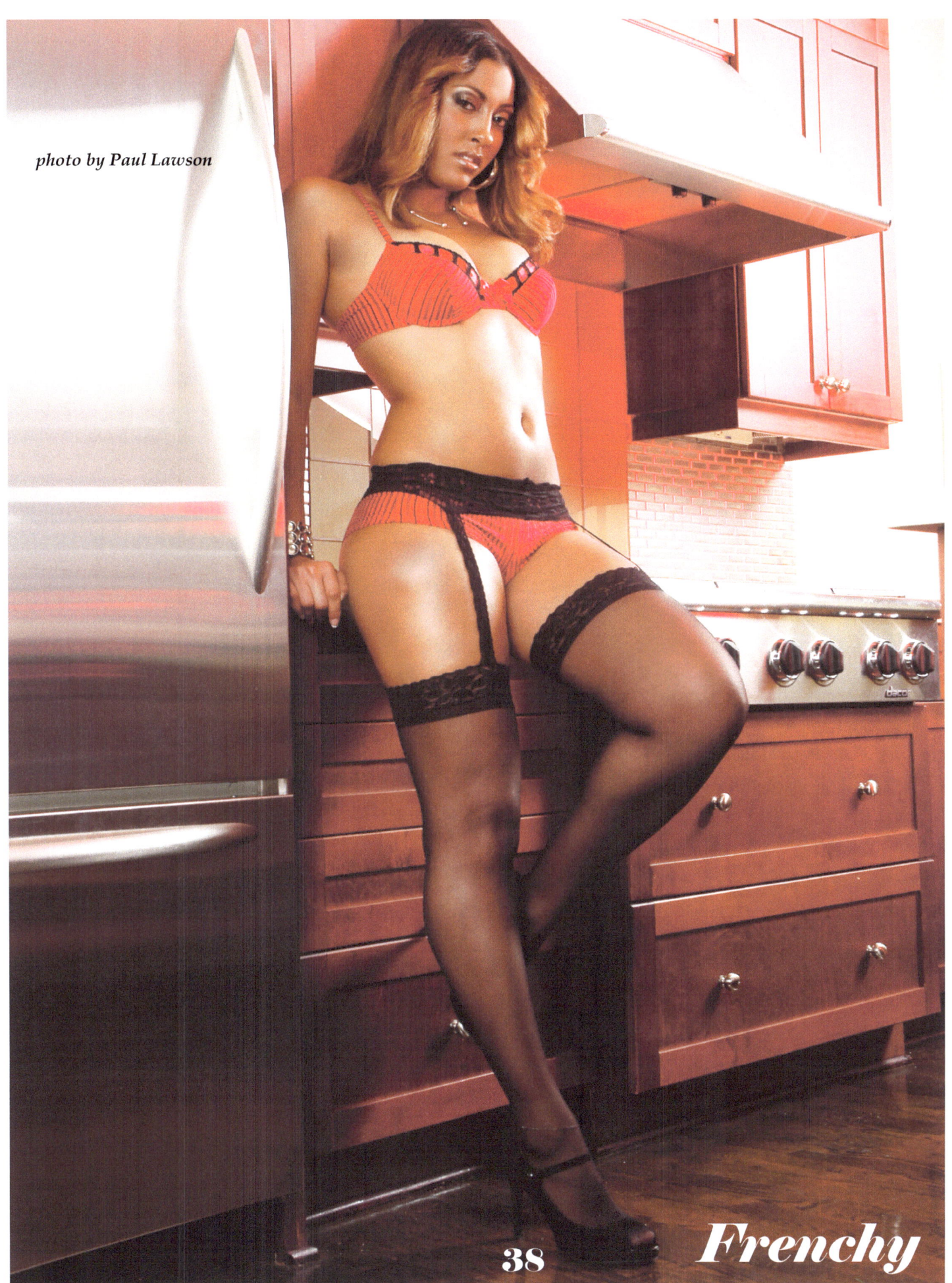

photo by Paul Lawson

Frenchy

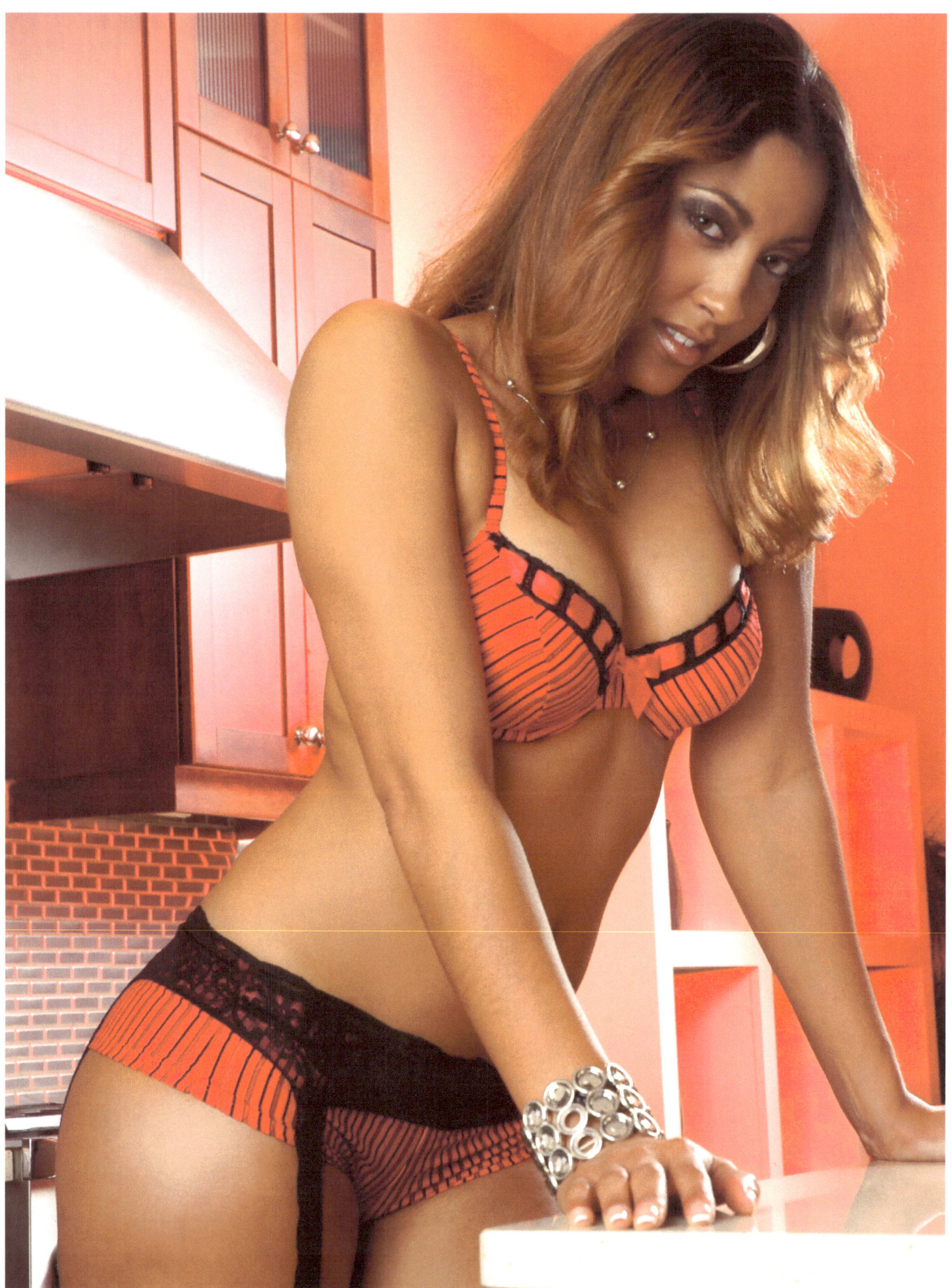

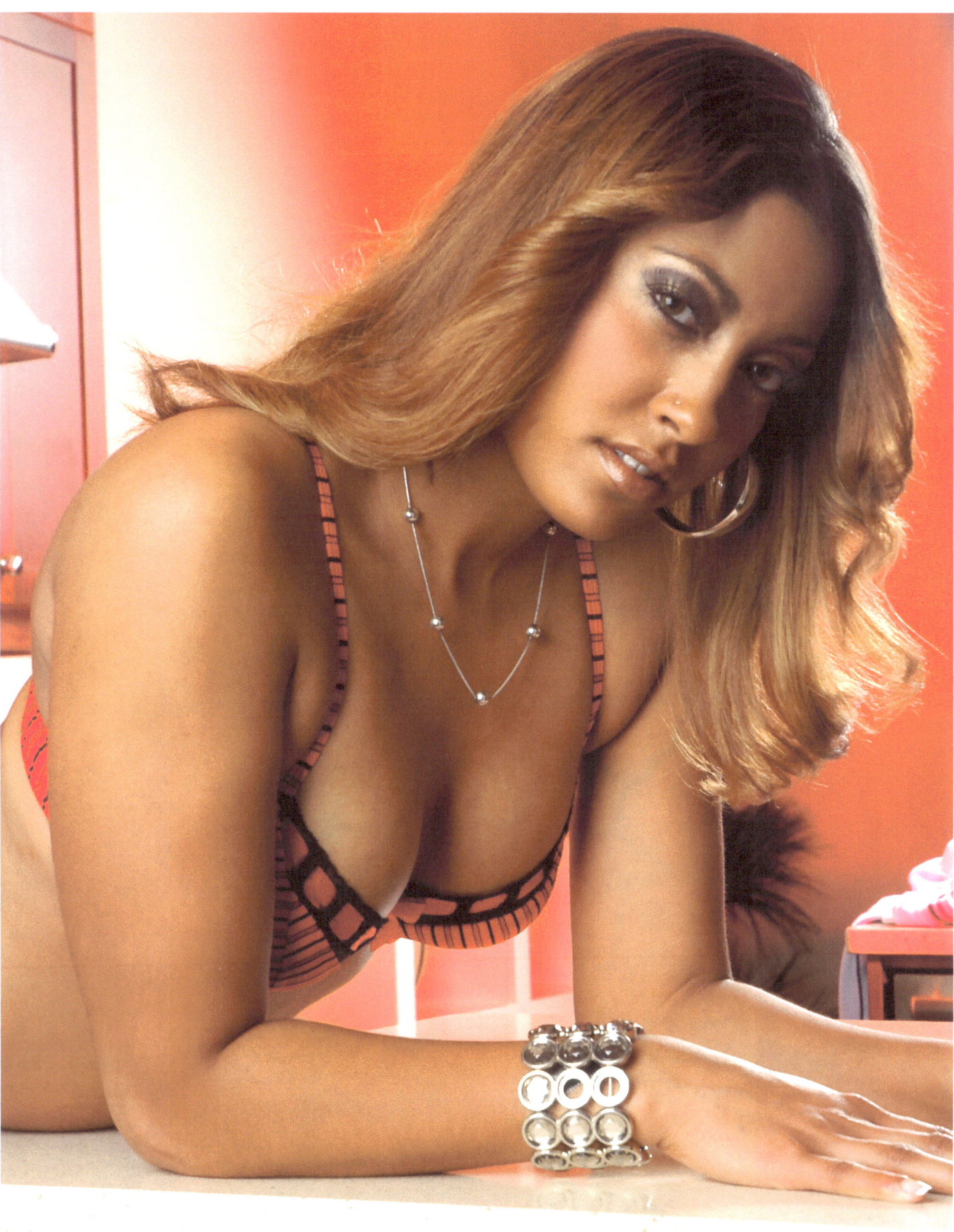

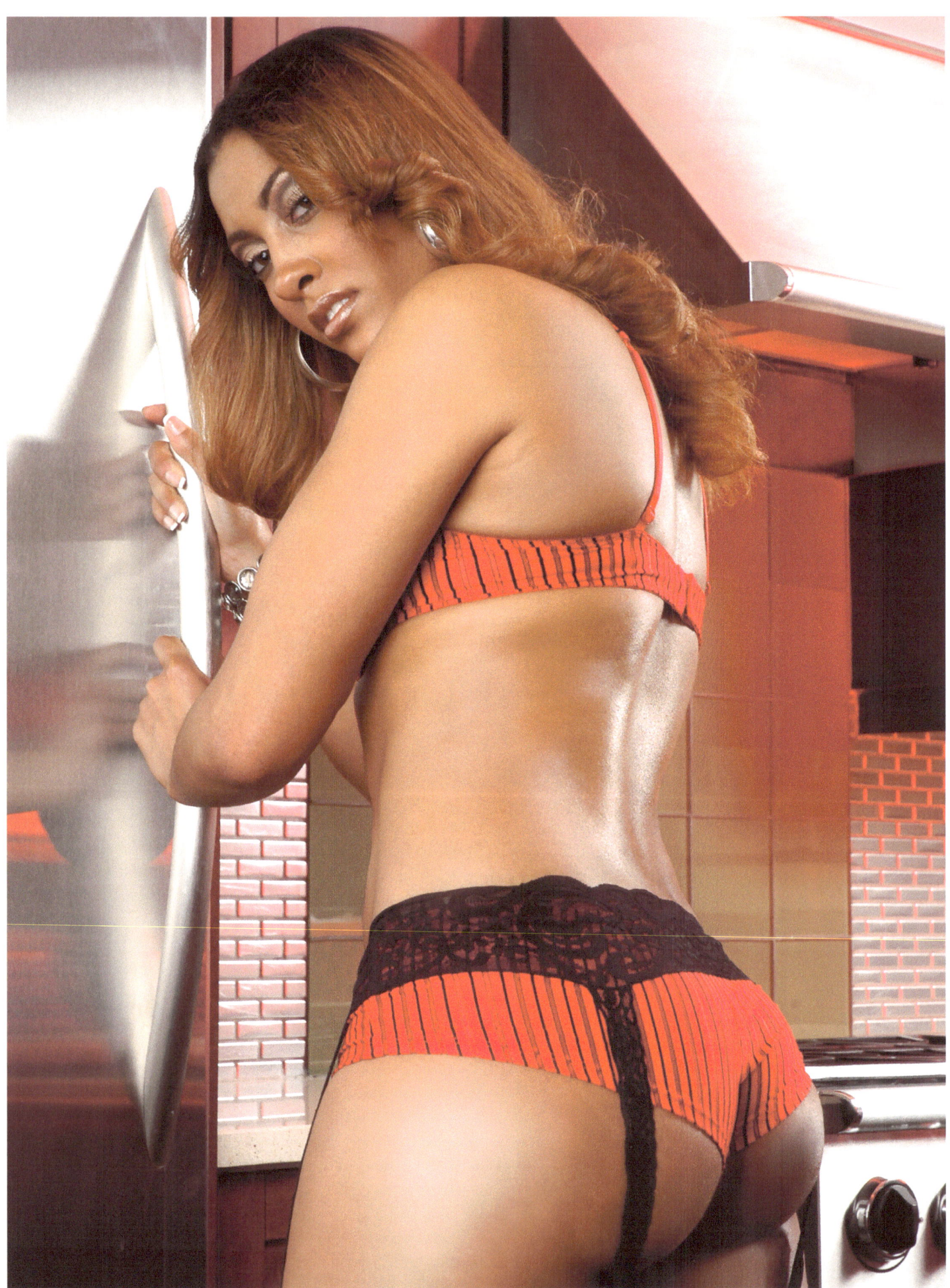

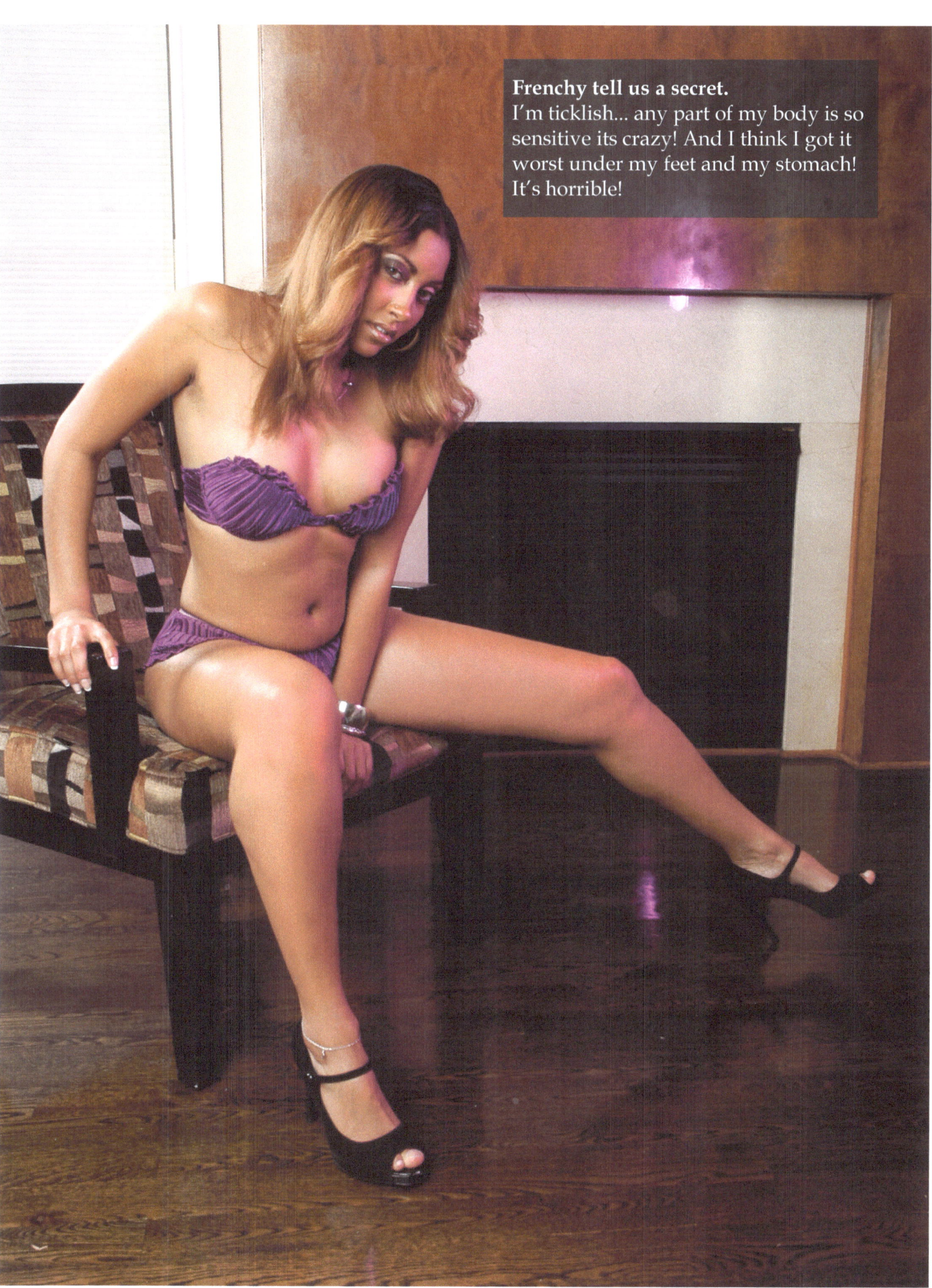

Frenchy tell us a secret.
I'm ticklish... any part of my body is so sensitive its crazy! And I think I got it worst under my feet and my stomach! It's horrible!

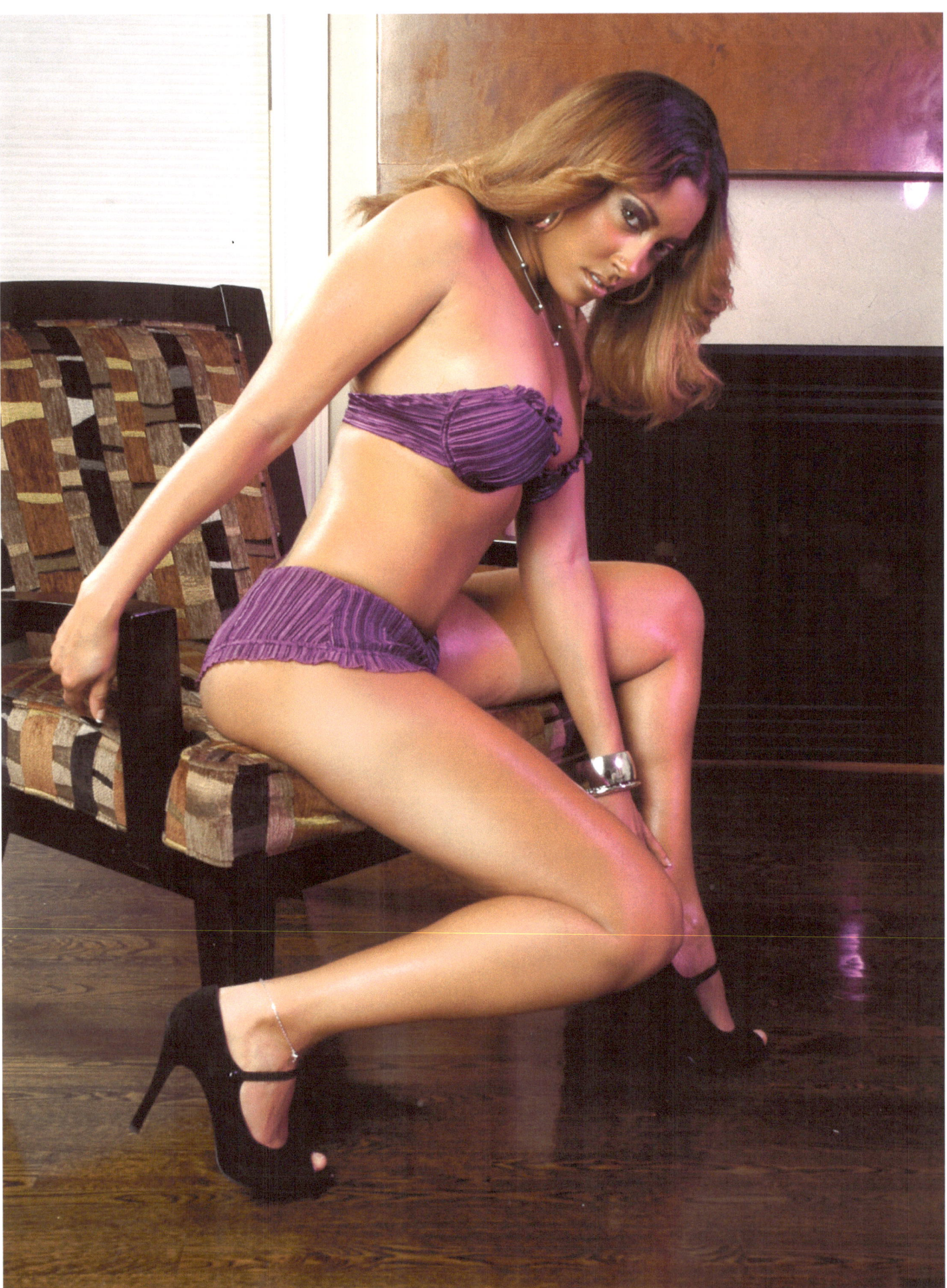